Devil's Advocates

DEVIL'S ADVOCATES is a series of books devoted to exploring the classics of horror cinema. Contributors to the series come from the fields of teaching, academia, journalism and fiction, but all have one thing in common: a passion for the horror film and a desire to share it with the widest possible audience.

'The admirable Devil's Advocates series is not only essential – and fun – reading for the serious horror fan but should be set texts on any genre course.'
Dr Ian Hunter, Reader in Film Studies, De Montfort University, Leicester

'Auteur Publishing's new Devil's Advocates critiques on individual titles... offer bracingly fresh perspectives from passionate writers. The series will perfectly complement the BFI archive volumes.' **Christopher Fowler,** *Independent on Sunday*

'Devil's Advocates has proven itself more than capable of producing impassioned, intelligent analyses of genre cinema... quickly becoming the go-to guys for intelligent, easily digestible film criticism.' **Horror Talk.com**

'Auteur Publishing continue the good work of giving serious critical attention to significant horror films.' **Black Static**

 DevilsAdvocatesbooks

 DevilsAdBooks

ALSO AVAILABLE IN THIS SERIES

A Girl Walks Home Alone at Night Farshid Kazemi

Black Sunday Martyn Conterio

The Blair Witch Project Peter Turner

Blood and Black Lace Roberto Curti

The Blood on Satan's Claw David Evans-Powell

Candyman Jon Towlson

Cannibal Holocaust Calum Waddell

Carrie Neil Mitchell

The Company of Wolves James Gracey

The Conjuring Kevin Wetmore

Creepshow Simon Brown

Cruising Eugenio Ercolani & Marcus Stiglegger

The Curse of Frankenstein Marcus K. Harmes

Daughters of Darkness Kat Ellinger

Dead of Night Jez Conolly & David Bates

The Descent James Marriot

The Devils Darren Arnold

Don't Look Now Jessica Gildersleeve

The Evil Dead Lloyd Haynes

The Fly Emma Westwood

Frenzy Ian Cooper

Halloween Murray Leeder

House of Usher Evert Jan van Leeuwen

In the Mouth of Madness Michael Blyth

It Follows Joshua Grimm

Ju-on The Grudge Marisa Hayes

Let the Right One In Anne Billson

M Samm Deighan

Macbeth Rebekah Owens

The Mummy Doris V. Sutherland

Nosferatu Cristina Massaccesi

Peeping Tom Kiri Bloom Walden

Re-Animator Eddie Falvey

Repulsion Jeremy Carr

Saw Benjamin Poole

Scream Steven West

The Shining Laura Mee

Shivers Luke Aspell

The Silence of the Lambs Barry Forshaw

Suspiria Alexandra Heller-Nicholas

The Texas Chain Saw Massacre James Rose

The Thing Jez Conolly

Trouble Every Day Kate Robertson

Twin Peaks: Fire Walk With Me Lindsay Hallam

The Witch Brandon Grafius

Witchfinder General Ian Cooper

FORTHCOMING

[REC] Jim Harper

Prevenge Andrew Graves

Scrooge Colin Fleming

Snuff Mark McKenna

Devil's Advocates

Cape Fear

Rob Daniel

ACKNOWLEDGEMENTS

They say no-one writes a book alone. That rings true here, and I have numerous people to thank. Firstly, *Cape Fear*'s screenwriter, Wesley Strick, who generously recounted his experiences on the film. His wit and insight improved both my understanding of the movie and the text in this book. Thanks also to Liz Parkinson at the BFI for providing audio materials from past lectures on Martin Scorsese. Images featured in the book would not have been as polished without the expert assistance of Michael Harrison. Ian Bird, Sarah Johnson, Robert Wallis, and Adrian Zak all suggested revisions and additions that made this a better book that it otherwise would have been. Any errors are mine alone. Huge thanks to John Atkinson at Auteur/LUP for supporting the project from inception, and making it a reality. This book is dedicated to my mum, who drove me to a cinema showing *Cape Fear* back in 1992, and who, to quote Barry Norman's review featured in this book, thought it was a "cracking good picture".

First published in 2021 by
Auteur, an imprint of
Liverpool University Press,
4 Cambridge Street,
Liverpool
L69 7ZU

Series design: Nikki Hamlett at Cassels Design
Set by Cassels Design, Luton UK

All rights reserved. No part of this publication may be reproduced in any material form (including photocopying or storing in any medium by electronic means and whether or not transiently or incidentally to some other use of this publication) without the permission of the copyright owner.

All illustrations from the 1991 *Cape Fear* are © Amblin Entertainment/Cappa Films/Tribeca Productions/Universal Pictures. Others are as indicated in the picture caption.

British Library Cataloguing-in-Publication Data
A catalogue record for this book is available from the British Library

ISBN paperback: 978-1-80085-702-5
ISBN hardback: 978-1-80085-701-8
ISBN epub: 978-1-80085-829-9
ISBN PDF: 978-1-80085-747-6

Contents

Synopsis 7

Introduction 9

Chapter 1: Scorsese and Horror Cinema 19

Chapter 2: Devil in the Details – Horror and *Cape Fear* 37

Chapter 3: Troubled Waters – Sexual Politics in *Cape Fear* 77

Chapter 4: Filmmaking at the Speed of Fear 99

Chapter 5: Legacy and Impact 109

Bibliography 121

SYNOPSIS

New Essex, North Carolina, 1991. Max Cady (Robert De Niro) is released from prison after serving fourteen years for rape and aggravated sexual battery. He begins a campaign of intimidation against Sam Bowden (Nick Nolte), the lawyer who defended him. He follows Sam, Sam's wife Leigh (Jessica Lange), and their fifteen-year-old daughter Danielle (Juliette Lewis) to a movie theatre and then to an ice cream parlour.

The following day, Cady reintroduces himself to Sam, muttering "You're gonna learn about loss." That night, Leigh spots Cady sitting on their garden wall. The next day, Sam confesses to a colleague that he was so appalled by Cady's crimes, he purposely buried evidence that showed the victim was promiscuous and may have consequently led to a lighter sentence or acquittal. Cady again confronts Sam, informing him that while imprisoned Cady became conversant with the law, and represented himself during various appeals. Sam's offer of money to Cady to leave town is rejected by the ex-con.

After the Bowden family dog is poisoned, Sam calls on police lieutenant Elgart (Robert Mitchum) to strongarm Cady into leaving town. When strip searching Cady the police discover he is covered with religious tattoos. They also learn he is independently wealthy, so are unable to bust him for vagrancy. He is released.

During a 4th of July parade, Cady goads Sam into attacking him by making lascivious comments about Leigh. In a bar, Cady picks up Lori (Illeana Douglas), a legal clerk with whom Sam has a flirtatious relationship. Cady attacks Lori in her apartment, biting a chunk from her cheek and raping her. Knowing she will be 'victim blamed' by Cady's defence team, a terrified Lori tells Sam she refuses to bring charges against the ex-con.

Sam becomes convinced Cady plans to rape Leigh and Danielle as revenge for his suppression of evidence back in 1977. Leigh accuses Sam, whose history of adultery meant they relocated to New Essex for a fresh start, of sleeping with Lori. Sam claims this is part of Cady's plan to create a rift between them, which will exacerbate tensions in the already dysfunctional household.

Sam hires private investigator Claude Kersek (Joe Don Baker) to tail Cady. The ex-con quickly realises he is being followed. Kersek's attempt to intimidate Cady into leaving New Essex fails.

Cady drives up to the road outside the Bowden's house and returns the family dog's collar to Leigh, claiming he found it. Leigh realises who he is and tells him how much he disgusts her. That evening, Cady calls Danielle, claiming to be her summer school drama teacher. He gives her advice on how to navigate adolescent awkwardness, and tells her their class has been moved to the school theatre. Danielle meets Cady in the theatre the next day, and realises he is the man her father warned her about. Cady convinces Danielle he means no harm, then subtly undermines her trust in her parents. He violates Danielle by slipping his thumb into her mouth and kissing her.

Having discovered a joint given to her by Cady, the Bowdens realise the ex-con came at Danielle. Sam agrees to Kersek's offer for three men to hospitalise Cady. Cady overcomes his attackers, then hires Lee Heller (Gregory Peck) to press charges against Sam, having previously recorded a conversation in which the lawyer threatened him.

Sam pretends to be away at a disbarment hearing, but remains home with his family and Kersek. Kersek plans to shoot Cady if he breaks into the house. Cady does break in, killing both Kersek and Sam's maid, Graciella (Zully Montero). The family flees, Sam telling Lt. Elgart they will return when Cady is found. But Cady attaches himself to their Jeep's undercarriage and attacks the family aboard their houseboat on the Cape Fear river.

After tying up Sam and putting Danielle in the hold, he attempts to rape Leigh, only stopping when she goes for his gun. He then releases Danielle in order to rape her and Leigh in front of Sam. While Cady is lighting a cigar, Danielle sprays him with lighter fluid she found in the hold. Aflame, Cady leaps into the river and Leigh and Danielle free Sam. Cady reappears on the boat and stages a mock trial, making Sam answer for failing to defend his client fourteen years earlier. Sam explains to his family he knew Cady was guilty of raping and battering his victim.

Cady tells Leigh and Danielle to strip, but the stormy waters of the river begin to rip the boat apart. Leigh and Danielle jump overboard, and Sam and Cady fight. Sam handcuffs Cady's foot to a railing in the houseboat before it is destroyed.

On the riverbank, Sam attempts to kill Cady, but the river sweeps the ex-con away and the wreckage pulls him underwater to his death. The family are reunited, but in voiceover Danielle says things will never be the same.

INTRODUCTION

> I set out to make a picture that was more mainstream and 'commercial', whatever that is… I mean, you can't – *I* can't – gauge what an audience is going to like and what's going to make money. There's no way. I just try to make the best picture I can.
> – Martin Scorsese, quoted in *Empire*, March 1992

Martin Scorsese's fourteenth film and first remake is a movie only *he* could have made. Granted, it is a reinterpretation of John D. MacDonald's 1957 novel *The Executioners* and J. Lee Thompson's 1962 screen adaptation, also titled *Cape Fear* and starring Gregory Peck as Sam Bowden and Robert Mitchum as Max Cady. But, the director's thematic preoccupations, personal baggage, dynamic formalism, and vast working knowledge of cinema are all present in what the opening credits proclaim is, 'A Martin Scorsese Picture'. More accurately, it should read, 'A Martin Scorsese *Horror* Picture'.

Yet, it all could have been so different. In 1989 this re-telling was intended to reach audiences as a Steven Spielberg film. Spielberg would have been no stranger to remakes; screenwriter Wesley Strick first met with him to discuss *Cape Fear* on the MGM lot, where the director was completing *Always* (1989), his reimagining of the Spencer Tracy vehicle *A Guy Named Joe* (Fleming, 1943).

In one sense, that Spielberg circled this dark, violent thriller is unsurprising. As the man behind *Duel* (1971) and *Jaws* (1975), his credentials as a suspense showman were beyond reproach. Despite having a reputation for sentimentality, depictions of fractious domestic life in *Close Encounters of the Third Kind* (1977) and *E.T. – The Extra Terrestrial* (1982) revealed a darker directorial view of suburban America. Scorsese's *Cape Fear* even shares minor parallels with Spielberg's 1972 TV movie *Something Evil*, in which a family discovers the wife has been targeted for possession by an unseen presence lurking within their newly bought farmhouse. A director seemingly unburdened by the sexual guilt Scorsese has often explored in his own work, it is intriguing to wonder how Steven Spielberg would have dramatised the sexual aggression at the centre of Max Cady's revenge. Most likely his interpretation would not have attracted the ire that greeted Scorsese's film from some critics upon release.

Accounts vary as to why Spielberg departed the project. In *De Niro: A Life*, author

Shawn Levy writes that post-production on *Hook* and pre-production on *Jurassic Park* forced Spielberg to drop the film from his schedule (2014, p.378). In a 1991 *New York Times* article, the director is quoted as saying, "I just couldn't find it inside me to make a scary movie about a family being preyed on by a maniac" (Maslin, 1991, p.14). What is accepted is Spielberg and Scorsese essentially swapped the properties they were lined up to direct. An adaptation of Thomas Kenneally's 1982 book *Schindler's Ark* was being prepped by Scorsese, but Spielberg talked his friend into relinquishing the rights so he himself could direct it as *Schindler's List* (1993) (Power, 2018).

Instead, Scorsese was persuaded to take *Cape Fear* to fulfill an agreement made with Universal Pictures. This was to be a 'one for them' assignment, made as a thank you to the studio after they bankrolled the ultimate 'one for me' film, *The Last Temptation of Christ* (1988). Although appearing to share few similarities, *Cape Fear* is a diabolical companion to the director's messiah picture. Both depict men struggling with a conflict between the flesh and the spirit, plus the painful road to salvation as a higher power forces them to confront their own natures. But, where Scorsese focused on Jesus in *The Last Temptation of Christ*, his attention was fixed on a Satanic figure in *Cape Fear*.

He was not just going to accept some anonymous studio assignment, however; a creative reason was required to take the gig. Motivation would not be found in the Bowdens, the family targeted by Max Cady. Scorsese read the script three times while editing *Goodfellas* (1990) and hated it: "The happy family was too much of a rose-tinted cliché. They were like Martians to me! Max was a bogeyman, and he was the one I sympathized with: let him get these sanctimonious prigs off our backs!" (Wilson, 2011, p.169).

Ironically, screenwriter Wesley Strick had also been reluctant to join the project. In interview, he told me he had disliked Thompson's original movie and, as a Jewish New Yorker, believed himself the wrong person to pen a script set in the South. But, despite outlining his misgivings to Spielberg in that meeting on the MGM lot, Strick stumbled out finding himself the film's scriptwriter. A first draft was delivered in November 1989, while Spielberg was still onboard, and would undergo twenty-four rewrites before Scorsese was happy. In Laurent Bouzereau's 2001 documentary *The Making of Cape Fear*, Strick recalls that Scorsese, "asked me to remove scores of details and moments and lines of dialogue. And almost every one I had put in with Steven Spielberg in mind." Explaining that he worked on a "smaller canvas", Scorsese collaborated with the writer in fleshing out the Bowdens' dysfunction (Bouzereau, 2001). But, even from draft one they were far removed from the apple pie family in J. Lee Thompson's 1962 film, according to Strick: "I dirtied up the Bowdens, and especially Sam, right away" (interview with author).

In the original film, described by Scorsese as a "perfect B-picture" (Bouzereau, 2001), Sam testified against Cady at his rape trial and secured his imprisonment. In the remake, Sam is recast as Cady's defence attorney, who suppresses evidence that Cady's victim was promiscuous after becoming convinced his client is guilty. From this ethical transgression and Sam's later infidelity, both occurring before the film begins, is created a maelstrom of family trauma. Scorsese wanted to dive deep into the dysfunction, particularly in the resentment Leigh feels for Sam, telling Strick, "Let's let them really go at it." Strick queried the number of pages this 'thriller' was dedicating to marital discord, explaining that "Jewish family fights last for three pages." Scorsese countered, "Well, Sicilian family fights are six pages" and won the argument (interview with author). Strick would be kept on throughout production, the first time the director had allowed this, to incorporate into the script extensive improvisation sessions between Robert De Niro, Jessica Lange, Nick Nolte, and Juliette Lewis. One plot event from the original film Strick recalls being told to retain was the houseboat climax (Bouzereau, 2001). Relocated from the Bowdens' house in the novel to the Cape Fear river, this also provides both film adaptations with their more evocative title (the Cape Fear river never being mentioned in *The Executioners*).

Someone committed to the project from the beginning was De Niro. While wrapping up acting duties on the McCarthy witch hunt movie *Guilty By Suspicion* (Winkler, 1991), he was prepping his next two films, *Backdraft* (Howard, 1991) and *Cape Fear* (Levy, 2014, p.372). De Niro's role as a fire investigator in *Backdraft* was essentially an extended cameo, and he devoted more time to developing Max Cady, although his scenes with Donald Sutherland's serial arsonist have the feel of a quick turnaround homage to *The Silence of the Lambs*, Jonathan Demme's shocker that had terrorised audiences earlier that year. It would be Scorsese's most famous onscreen alter-ego who persuaded the director to accept *Cape Fear* as his next movie: "'Bob leaned down at the table,' recalls Scorsese, smiling at the memory. 'He knelt beside me, took my ear, and said, 'We could *do* something with this guy, you know?'" (Gleiberman, 1992, p.64).

Robert De Niro has a habit of dragging his friend to projects that contribute to the director's reputation as a master filmmaker. *Raging Bull* (1980), *The King of Comedy* (1982) and *The Irishman* (2019) are other projects De Niro persuaded him to accept. In July 1990, he and Spielberg organised a script read in New York to convince Scorsese to join *Cape Fear*. De Niro played Cady, Kevin Kline was Sam, Patricia Clarkson read for Leigh (when the character was still named Karen), and Moira Kelly was Danielle (Levy, 2014, p.378), although in *The Making of Cape Fear*, Strick recalls Kline's wife Phoebe Cates playing the daughter....The production company credits opening the film speak to its evolution, with Spielberg's Amblin Entertainment, Scorsese's Cappa Films, and De Niro's Tribeca Productions all 'presenting' the movie.

As he had done with *Raging Bull*, De Niro began an exercise regime to portray a character at peak physical fitness. Robert Mitchum's Cady in the 1962 original is a brawny, barrel-chested menace; De Niro's incarnation is a 5% body fat weapon, biblical tattoos adorning his ripped torso. The actor also elected to spend $5,000 making his teeth crooked to give Cady the look of someone from a breadline background, then a further $20,000 fixing them after shooting had wrapped. Nick Nolte was cast in the Gregory Peck role as Sam Bowden. Nolte had been the lead in *Life Lessons*, Scorsese's segment of the 1989 portmanteau film *New York Stories*, with Francis Ford Coppola and Woody Allen providing the other two sections. Other actors mooted for Bowden had included Warren Beatty and Robert Redford (both also considered as directors), plus Mel Gibson, Clint Eastwood, Robin Williams, John Lithgow, and Liam Neeson (Levy, 2014, p.378). The latter would cameo for Scorsese as a supportive father to Leonardo DiCaprio in 2002's *Gangs of New York*, and star as a less supportive Father in 2016's *Silence*.

Jessica Lange took the role of Leigh primarily to work with De Niro and Scorsese, having missed out on the role of Vickie in *Raging Bull* to Cathy Moriarty. Lange worked extensively with Strick to improve the role, and at the time of production told the *Los Angeles Times*, "I don't think they really planned on addressing the character until they knew who was going to play it" (Morgan, 1991a). Hopefuls for the role of Bowden daughter Danielle included Moira Kelly, Fairuza Balk and, according to Shawn Levy in *De Niro: A Life*, Illeana Douglas. Douglas would instead play Lori, the legal clerk with whom Sam has a flirtatious friendship and Cady's savaged onscreen victim. Danielle would go to Juliette Lewis, the first actor who auditioned for the part (Bouzereau, 2001). Lewis had prior experience portraying a daughter trapped in a dysfunctional family, having appeared in *National Lampoon's Christmas Vacation* (Chechik, 1989).

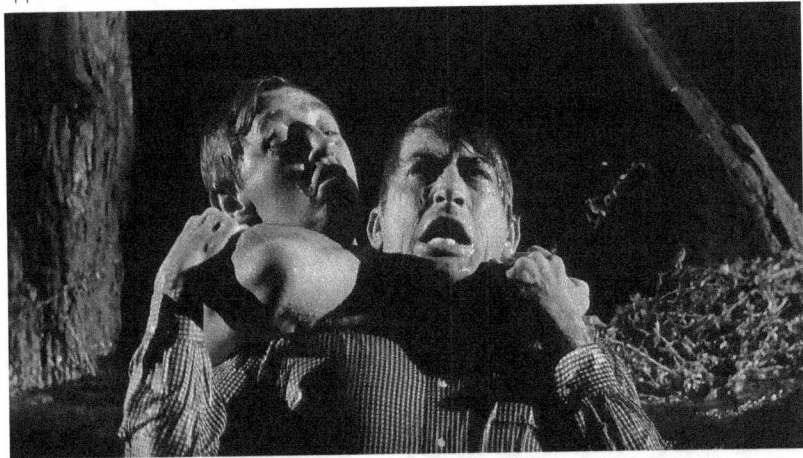

Fig. 1 Robert Mitchum and Gregory Peck in 1962's Cape Fear... © Melville-Talbot Productions

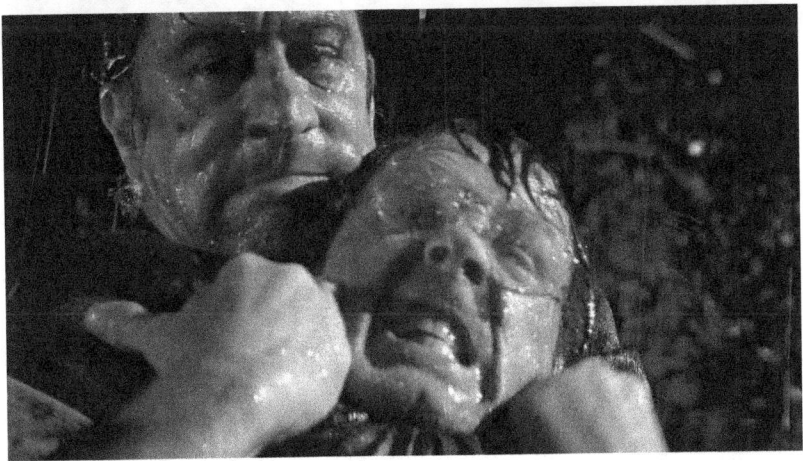

Fig. 2 ...and Robert De Niro and Nick Nolte in Scorsese's version © Melville-Talbot Productions

Shooting began in November 1990, a year after Strick delivered his first draft, and wrapped in March 1991. Following test audience feedback, a few days of reshoots were added to clarify moments during the climax. Principal photography occurred in Fort Lauderdale, with Florida doubling for North Carolina. To sell the illusion, North Carolina's distinctive moss was hung from trees in the Bowdens' garden. The Bowdens' house was real, not a set, which proved a challenge for a director used to break away walls and ceilings to allow for the exact angles he wanted. A courthouse scene was shot in Miami. The houseboat climax was filmed in a specially constructed 90ft tank in Fort Lauderdale, with miniatures shot on the H Stage in Shepperton Studios, Surrey, UK.

Scorsese recruited Freddie Francis as Director of Photography. The horror director and legendary cinematographer of such films as *The Innocents* (Clayton, 1961) and *The Elephant Man* (Lynch, 1980) was brought on board for his "...instinct and deep knowledge from the suspense and horror films he worked on" (Thompson/Christie, 1996, p.171). Thelma Schoonmaker edited the film, as she has done with every Scorsese narrative feature since *Raging Bull*. Her professional relationship with the director had begun far earlier, editing his debut movie *Who's That Knocking at My Door* (1967). Elaine and Saul Bass created a credit sequence that introduces the film's themes and atmosphere, described by Scorsese as a "mini-movie that precedes the picture" (Bouzereau, 2001). The late Bernard Herrmann's score from the original film was used again in the remake. Elmer Bernstein, famed composer of many movies including *The Great Escape* (Sturges, 1963) and *An American Werewolf in London* (Landis, 1981), was recruited to rearrange Herrmann's music and give it a sonic overhaul. Bernstein would write approximately six minutes of new material to bridge gaps in the cues, and incorporate tracks from Herrmann's unused score for Alfred Hitchcock's *Torn Curtain* (1966) during the houseboat climax.

Cape Fear was premiered in New York on Sunday 6th October 1991, less than thirteen months after *Goodfellas'* NYC premiere in 1990. On Friday 15th November the film went on general release in the US, and in the UK on Friday 6th March 1992. Beyond being his introduction to the world of remakes, for Martin Scorsese this was a film of other firsts: The first straight genre movie he had attempted; his first picture using the 2.39:1 aspect ratio; the first time he had tackled major action set pieces and employed miniatures and CGI. *Cape Fear* was also Scorsese's first bona fide blockbuster, grossing

$79m in the United States and a total $182m globally off a c.$35m budget. This box office haul would be his biggest until *Gangs of New York*'s $194m over a decade later, but the protracted shooting and editing schedules for that movie left it, and Scorsese, in the red.

Cape Fear was also the director's first horror film, although the genre label was not typically applied, least of all by Scorsese himself. In Michael Henry Wilson's *Cahiers du Cinema* book *Scorsese on Scorsese*, the filmmaker said, "(Audiences) expect powerful sensations because that's part of the thriller genre. You can't deny them that, but you can perhaps find a way of getting around it" (2011, p.169).

The Scorsese way of "getting around it" moved *Cape Fear* far from the glossy excitement of a Hollywood thriller. As I shall explore, his approach to the material and his famous Catholic lens dovetailed with trends in contemporary horror cinema. One year before Quentin Tarantino popularised the term by grounding his whole aesthetic in it, Scorsese delivered a ferociously postmodern work, a cine-literate pastiche of mainstream thrillers, with the director looking to movies that had provided formative shocks, and recruiting personnel from the Classical Hollywood period. The result is a film that plays as if Scorsese imagined his audience to be Alfred Hitchcock, Val Lewton and Mario Bava.

Upon the film's release, popular reviews played fast and loose with genre-specific language. While few called it a horror film, quotes plastered on posters giddily announced the terror that awaited those brave enough to buy a ticket. In *Rolling Stone*, Peter Travers wrote, "Martin Scorsese unleashes a series of shocks that will leave you breathless." "Stay away if you're squeamish," warned Vincent Canby in *The New York Times*. "See *Cape Fear* with someone you want to hold onto… tight," declared no less an authority than Piers Morgan in *The Sun*. "[M]ore scary than *Silence of the Lambs*," promised Drew MacKenzie in the *Daily Mirror*. The *Silence of the Lambs* comparison is particularly relevant. Demme's multi-Oscar winner is another example of a thriller that, due to its visual style, sound design and approach to plot, reads more comfortably as a horror film. Like *Jaws* and *Psycho* (Hitchcock, 1960), *Cape Fear* and *The Silence of the Lambs* are movies that terrified audiences, but whose fluid approach to genre places them across multiple categories. In 1995, David Fincher's *Seven* would join their ranks.

While Scorsese was breaking new ground with *Cape Fear*, in other ways it was a continuation, most notably in the controversy the film received upon release, particularly in the US. The director was no stranger to passionate and passionately negative reactions to his movies. Critics had decried both the casting of a 12-year-old Jodie Foster as a child prostitute in *Taxi Driver* (1976), and the graphic violence during that film's climax. *The Last Temptation of Christ*, adapted from Nikos Kazantzakis's pilloried 1955 novel, had drawn down the ire of the United States' Christian right. They pressured Paramount Pictures into dropping the film from its production slate in 1983, picketed new studio Universal Pictures, and lambasted the movie sight unseen when it was finally released in 1988. *Goodfellas*, Scorsese's film before *Cape Fear* and an unexpected sleeper hit, was attacked for purportedly glamourising the lifestyle, and thereby endorsing the character, of mobster Henry Hill.

But *Cape Fear* was different. Scorsese had received criticism for the depiction of women in previous films, but certain commentators read the gender politics here as cause for alarm. Although critiquing character motivations and events from both *The Executioners* and the original 1962 film, the remake nonetheless features an antagonist who uses rape to exact revenge after serving prison time for the same crime. This brings it close to the rape-revenge narrative present in film since the early days of cinema, and which rose to become a recognised sub-genre from the 1970s onwards, following the success of films such as *Straw Dogs* (Peckinpah, 1971), *Deliverance* (Boorman, 1972), *The Last House on the Left* (Craven, 1972) and *Death Wish* (Winner, 1974). Often told from a rightwing perspective, in a rape-revenge narrative the sexual attack on a female character initiates a crusade, typically for the male lead (boyfriend or husband or family member, usually a father), who embraces biblical justice. There may be handwringing on the protagonist's part as he sacrifices nobler characteristics to defeat his nemesis, but the film's politics will affirm as necessary this temporary acceptance of vigilantism.

While technically not true examples of the rape-revenge narrative, all versions of the *Cape Fear* story share plot and character psychology crossovers. Both film adaptations resultantly drew criticism for their depiction of sexual threat and sexual violence. The 1962 version was cut by a reported six-minutes to secure a UK release, much to the chagrin of director J. Lee Thompson (Norman, 1962, p.3). In the UK, the original film received an uncut home video release in early 1992, capitalising on the remake's publicity. An indication of the change in times was that Scorsese avoided the pre-release problems Thompson encountered, Strick telling me: "I don't recall Universal ever inserting themselves into the process or trying to get us to compromise." Similarly, both the US and UK ratings boards passed the 1991 film uncut. But, some critical commentary saw Scorsese as overstepping the mark in his depiction of sexual terrorisation.

In the April 1992 issue of *Sight and Sound*, Pam Cook wrote that the film's female characters are attracted to their rapist and collude "in their own humiliation". She closes the article arguing: "Scorsese has produced his most overtly femino-phobic movie. We can hardly thank him for that. At the most, we can thank him for laying on the line with blistering clarity the way our culture devalues femininity as an alibi for male fears and desires" (1992, p.15). The February 1992 issue of Empire outlined the controversy raging in the US, in a feature entitled 'Who's Afraid of *Cape Fear*': "…Scorsese is suddenly being blasted for the alleged misogyny and violence inflicted against women in *Cape Fear*, being specifically taken to task for the general swipe his film takes at the current wave of 'political correctness' in the US, a movement currently sweeping through college campuses across the country… some critics are now citing *Cape Fear* as Scorsese's own personal backlash against the entire feminist/PC movement in the US" (1992, p.6).

The film does contain sexual violence, the result of Robert De Niro's typically extensive research, that continues to shock audiences. The hysteria of the violence is enhanced by the style in which it is depicted, marrying the kineticism of *Goodfellas* with the heated delirium of Southern Gothic. But, what was the director's intent when accepting the gig of helming *Cape Fear*?

Here is a filmmaker renowned for intensely personal works, who typically subsumes political commentary into his characters' psychologies. Despite the presence of a presidential hopeful in *Taxi Driver*, the film is an expressionistic depiction of insanity, rather than a sociological study of the intersection between mental illness, violence and government policy. Any critique of the American health care system in *Bringing Out the Dead* (1999) is implied, while the film focusses on the spiritual anguish of Nicolas Cage's paramedic. When introducing a political element to *Gangs of New York*, the uneven, confused storytelling speaks to Scorsese's lack of interest in the subject. 2019's *The*

Irishman was more successful in its retelling of post-war American politics, primarily due to couching its discussion in the language of gangster cinema.

Arguably therefore, a "personal backlash against the entire feminist/PC movement in the US" seems to be something beyond the interest of the director, and his subsequent films do not appear to have continued a specific agenda in this area. Yet, Cook's comment of "male fears and desires" taps into a central Scorsese concern: an exploration of tortured masculinity and toxic machismo. Exploration of this within a more commercial setting seemed to power Scorsese's interest in *Cape Fear*, and Cook's claim that this relates to a femino-phobia will be analysed.

While *Cape Fear* did meet with glowing critical praise upon release, it also saw the business end of damning notices for failing more generally. Joel Siegel on *Good Morning America* cited the film as proof that "Martin Scorsese is the greatest American director" (poster quote). But, in *The New Yorker*, Terence Rafferty labelled the film "a disgrace", declaring, "It's hard to find the pleasure, or value, in a horror picture that keeps providing us with high-toned justifications for our basest reactions — insisting that the grueling experience it's putting us through is really meant to edify us" (Rafferty, 1991). Agreeing with Joel Siegel's assessment, Matt Mueller's 5-star review in *Empire* asserted, "…with *Cape Fear*, Scorsese solidifies his position as America's greatest living filmmaker" (Mueller, 1992, p.17). In the *Chicago Reader*, Jonathan Rosenbaum offered a negative assessment: "It's hard to understand why Martin Scorsese wanted to remake a nasty, formulaic 1962 thriller whose only 'classic' credentials are a terrifying performance by Robert Mitchum and a Bernard Herrmann score" (Rosenbaum, 1991).

Another of the film's critics is Martin Scorsese himself. In Tom Shone's *Scorsese: A Retrospective*, he is quoted as saying, "The films I make are very personal films… I think it requires a great deal of humility to make a thriller and I can't do that. I promised Universal I'd make them a picture. I'm not excusing the film; I tried a lot of things with it – some successful, some not – and quite honestly I don't know if it works or not" (Shone, 2014, p.158).

Apt then that this critical analysis is for the 'Devil's Advocates' series, pleading a case for the defence.

Chapter 1: Scorsese and Horror Cinema

> Somebody once wrote, I think a British critic, if you don't really understand or appreciate the horror genre, you really have no love or understanding of film itself. – Martin Scorsese, interviewed on *Late Night with David Letterman*, February 1982

Scorsese famously said his whole life is movies and religion. His incorporation of horror themes and imagery into his work can usefully be viewed in connection to both.

The Horror of Scorsese's Cinema

In 2015, website *The Daily Beast* invited Martin Scorsese to share his scariest films of all time. The list of 11 movies he supplied offers insight into the director's formative shocks, plus the thematic concerns of those chillers that would influence his work, including *Cape Fear*.

1. *The Haunting* (Wise, 1963)
2. *Isle of the Dead* (Robson, 1945)
3. *The Uninvited* (Allen, 1944)
4. *The Entity* (Furie, 1982)
5. *Dead of Night* (Cavalcanti, Crichton, Dearden, Hamer, 1945)
6. *The Changeling* (Medak, 1980)
7. *The Shining* (Kubrick, 1980)
8. *The Exorcist* (Friedkin, 1973)
9. *Night of the Demon* (Tourneur, 1957)
10. *The Innocents* (Clayton, 1961)
11. *Psycho* (Hitchcock, 1960)

Scorsese was asked to name his scariest movies of all time. Whether he would have answered differently had he been requested to list the *best* horror films of all time is a tantalising thought. Despite the lack of international cinema on the list, it reveals that the director who said, "I'd like horror to be taken more seriously" (Thompson/Christie, 1996, p.101) draws inspiration from diverse cinematic shockers, sometimes in unlikely places. The one surprising omission is Michael Powell's *Peeping Tom* (1960), for which Scorsese spearheaded a restoration that premiered at a Museum of Modern Art retrospective on Powell and Emeric Pressburger in New York in 1980.

Using the list as a basis for what informs the director's sense of horror, the fundamental question of whether evil exists as its own entity, or is it in man's nature to be evil, figures prominently. *Cape Fear* wrestled with this as part of its recalibration of Sam's moral code from previous versions. It also insists the audience does likewise in placing Sam's actions against the danger posed by Cady. Here we see Scorsese's thematic obsessions dovetailing with those of horror cinema: guilt, sin, penance, redemption and the impossibility of redemption, psychosis, and psychosexual dread. He frequently illustrates these themes through depictions of bodily destruction, evoking sensations most often found in horror. Notice how many titles on that list of eleven deal with those same themes, and note also the recurrence of that cornerstone convention of the horror movie, a family undergoing crisis.

Scorsese said he recruited *The Innocents*' cinematographer Freddie Francis for *Cape Fear* due to the Englishman's "understanding of the concept of the Gothic atmosphere" (Morgan, 1991b). Gothic cinema made an impact on the young Scorsese, particularly American International Pictures' Edgar Allan Poe movies, directed by Roger Corman and starring Vincent Price. Scorsese cites *The Fall of the House of Usher* (Corman, 1960) as important to his peer group for the "beautiful atmosphere in its use of colour and Cinemascope. We loved this blend of English Gothic and French *grand guignol*, mixed together in an American film" (Thompson/Christie, 1996, p.20).

Corman would give Scorsese his first professional movie, hiring him to direct indie exploitation picture *Boxcar Bertha* (1972). A *Bonnie and Clyde* (Penn, 1967) rip-off intended as a follow-up to AIP's *Bloody Mama* (Corman, 1970), *Boxcar Bertha* provided a crash course in commercial filmmaking. Corman allowed the young Scorsese to "test his radical, aesthetic ambitions against the discipline of genre imperatives and audience reaction" (Thompson/Christie, 1996, p.xix). Good grounding for putting thematic and emotional meat onto the skeleton of the Hollywood thriller in *Cape Fear* years later. As a thank you to Corman, Scorsese would include a scene from *The Tomb of Ligeia* (Corman, 1964) in *Mean Streets* (1973). The scene features a character being consumed in flames, small comfort to the street criminals seeking solace in a cinema when real-life danger presses in. *Mean Streets*' original title, 'Season of the Witch', also belies a fondness for Gothic horror…and the music of Donovan, whose song 'Atlantis' would years later counterpoint a vicious beating in *Goodfellas*.

Many of the director's thematic concerns appear within Gothic fiction. Therefore, it is understandable that his approach to depicting fear should synch with formative Gothic author Ann Radcliffe's three definitions: the physical and mental terror of pain and death, the horror when perceiving something as evil or morally repugnant, and the mystery of encountering something beyond explanation (Monléon, 1990, p.11).

Mystery, which we shall refer to as 'the uncanny', is particularly applicable to Scorsese, with those inexplicable experiences being "…thereby productive of a nameless apprehension that may be called religious dread in the face of the wholly other" (quoted in Monléon, 1990, p.11). While ostensibly a director fixed in recognisably real worlds, the uncanny bleeds into Scorsese's work. The religious dread in his films suggests unseen, unfriendly forces. But, often these orchestrating powers are explained as a character's delusion or psychosis, making Scorsese's men heirs to Norman Bates' mantle. *Cape Fear* is his film that most embraces the uncanny. Like many titles on the list (*The Haunting*, *The Innocents*, *The Shining*, segments of *Dead of Night*), it does not wholly reconcile its central tension. The audience must decide whether Cady is merely psychotic, or imbued with the power and authority of a higher agency.

Paranoia seeps into most films on that list of eleven, often fuelled by the uncanny. The superstitions that grip a plague ridden island in *Isle of the Dead*. The fear of something inexplicable taking over characters' lives in *Dead of Night*, or threatening loved ones as in *The Innocents*. A husband's rage when suspecting his wife of undermining his ambitions in *The Shining*. Paranoia impedes redemption, and characters are destroyed by their own fears, something Scorsese explored in 1963's *What's a Nice Girl Like You Doing In a Place Like This?*, his first student movie, which he described as a film of "pure paranoia"

(Thompson/Christie, 1996, p.15). Laced with mordant wit, it features the character of Algernon (Zeph Michaelis) as the first of many Scorsese obsessives. Algernon's life crumbles after he becomes fixated on a photograph of a figure in a rowboat on a lake. Perhaps the figure in the photo is responsible; it is after all Scorsese in his first cameo. Delusions of persecution and betrayal blight many Scorsese males, none more so than *Raging Bull*'s Jake La Motta, who spies marital infidelity in every look and comment. The director claims La Motta is more accepting of himself come the movie's close, but his existence still appears purgatorial.

"Guilt. There is nothing you can tell me about guilt," Scorsese once said during a conversation with Roger Ebert and Paul Schrader (Ebert, 2008, p.43). Unsurprisingly, guilt, and its mischievous cousin sin, are present in all eleven films on the list, be they tales of dead family members returning to uncover a terrible past crime (*The Changeling*, *The Uninvited*), a family ripping itself apart (*The Shining*), or destructive manias created by repressed sexuality (*The Innocents*, *Psycho*, *The Haunting*). Sexual dread also looms heavy and foreboding. *The Shining*'s woman in room 237 can be seen as the product of a guilty mind recoiling at the consequences of adulterous urges. *The Exorcist* remains disturbing in large part due to its corruption of sexuality through abasement and self-mutilation. William Friedkin's influential shocker would also play a part in bringing Scorsese into the industry; due to the film's success, *The Exorcist* star Ellen Burstyn had the freedom to make 1974's *Alice Doesn't Live Here Anymore*, and hire a relatively unknown Scorsese as director. *Alice*'s commercial success and a Best Actress Oscar for Burstyn cemented the director's status in Hollywood.

Sexual terror is the bedrock of *The Entity*. This "based on true events" horror film, about a woman's sexual abuse at the hands of a poltergeist, has a visual flamboyance that seems to inform *Cape Fear*. The film's treatment of sexual violence as a means of exploring male weakness and control also aligns with Scorsese's remake, but did not draw as much critical anger. This is possibly due to its fantastical nature, along with mainstream attitudes of the time; *The Entity* blends elements of the devil and rape-revenge films, both of which were drawing sizeable audiences in the early 1980s. The film also benefits from Barbara Hershey's sensitive lead performance. Hershey had previously played the title character in Scorsese's *Boxcar Bertha*, and would later portray Mary Magdalene in *The Last Temptation of Christ*.

Fig. 3 Dynamic framing in The Entity © *American Cinema Productions*

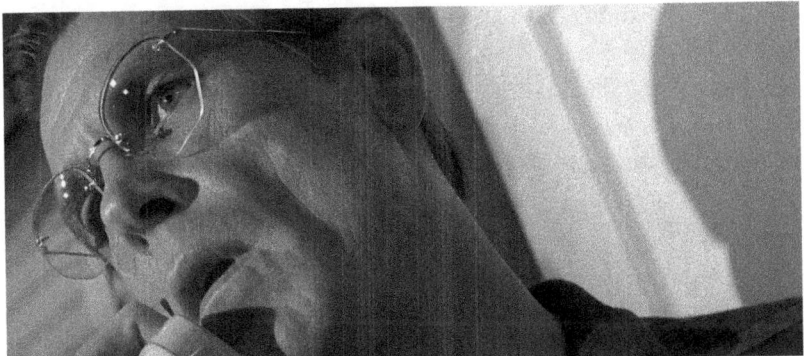

Fig. 4 A similarly canted view of the world in Cape Fear

From Scorsese's earliest output, sexual dread bubbled beneath and frequently broke the surface. When horror movie distributor Joseph Brenner offered him $37,000 to complete *Who's That Knocking at My Door*, the filmmaker complied with Brenner's proviso that he include a sex scene. The extra sequence is a fantasy, featuring Harvey Keitel's character J.R. and a series of brunette women… all set to the Oedipal section of The Doors track, 'The End'. This sexual dread takes on near-mythic proportions in *After Hours* (1985), Scorsese's (arguably) first foray into fantastical feature filmmaking. While in a café reading Henry Miller's *The Tropic of Cancer* (from which the film's story will draw loose inspiration), Paul (Griffin Dunne) begins a conversation with Marcy (Roseanna Arquette). On the promise of a bagel-shaped paperweight and the suggestion of a more intimate encounter, Paul journeys down to Marcy's SoHo apartment. But a night of frustrated expectations and misunderstandings sees him wrongly accused of being a burglar terrorising the neighbourhood. The vigilante mob that takes to the streets to catch him recalls the pitchfork branding villagers of *Frankenstein* (Whale, 1931). The coincidences and contrivances that prevent Paul leaving SoHo become near cosmic. On the film's audio commentary, Scorsese describes the characters as "mythological in some way," adding "I always liked the character from Greek mythology going across the river to Hades. But he has no money to pay the boatman." Here, Paul loses the $20 with which he was going to pay a cab driver, so like those mythical penniless souls is condemned to wander this underworld.

The paranoia Paul feels in Scorsese's *After Hours* often stems from women. A sense of punishment for his impure thoughts is ever-present, plus a fear of, and bafflement in, the opposite sex. In the director's words, "You think you're going to heaven, but it's hell that awaits you!" (Wilson, 2011, p.123). Joe Minion was a postgraduate student at Columbia University when he penned the script, but the then-fortysomething Scorsese confessed to sympathising with Paul's "erotic difficulties" (Wilson, 2011, p.123). In this world, women are an unknowable, sometimes monstrous Other. Paul becomes obsessed with the idea Marcy is scarred with burns after misreading clues (ointment, a medical journal), and a childhood memory of being alone in a hospital burn ward. In *The Scorsese Connection*, Lesley Stern writes, "There is the idea of woman as wound (or rather the idea of female lips, genitalia as wound), and woman as… potentially lethal" (1995, p.109). Stern ties this back to the tension between the supernatural and explainable: "And, each time, the woman is uncannily familiar, indicating the female lips/wound as curiously *unheimlich*" (1995, p.109).

This sense of the *unheimlich*, the tension between the rational and unexplainable, was even more prominent and monstrously fantastic in the script's outrageously Freudian original climax. A maternal figure grows to huge proportions and Paul seeks safety inside her. Producer David Geffen said *no*, so Paul was instead transformed into a frozen paper mâché sculpture by Verna Bloom's unnervingly maternal artist. It was Michael Powell who suggested the film's circular fairy-tale style ending, with Paul abducted and winding up back at his office. Peter Jackson would later explore that original ending's imagery in the memorable splatterfest *Brain Dead* (1993).

When Paul flicks through the medical journal, glimpsing images of burn victims, the scene employs the visual language of horror: low angle camerawork, key light on the eyes, deep shadow background. On the *After Hours* audio commentary, cinematographer Michael Ballhaus says, "The movie sometimes looked like a horror movie… sometimes it was important that it was scary. It was in a way realistic and it had this touch of the surreal. That gave it a very interesting thrill. It was Marty's way of doing things."

"Marty's way of doing things" often draws upon horror aesthetics…

Psycho, film number 11 on the list, looms over much of Scorsese's work. Bernard Herrmann reprised the final musical notes from Hitchcock's shocker for the closing moments of *Taxi Driver*, completing the score the day he died. While shooting *Cape Fear*, the director said, "(I) constantly had Herrmann's music in my head – that of the first *Cape Fear* but especially *Psycho*" (Thompson/Christie, 1996, p.173). Saul Bass, designer of *Psycho*'s jagged opening credits sequence, approximates the font for *Cape Fear*'s credits. The close-up of Norman Bates' eye peering through a spyhole at Marion undressing is referenced in both *Goodfellas*, as the young Henry Hill observes the gangsters on the street below, and in *Cape Fear* when Danielle watches Cady's attempted rape of her mother. Scorsese uses the shot in two moments that denote a child's end of innocence, which may provide insight into how he views Norman Bates. Jake La Motta's bloody final fight with Sugar Ray Robinson in *Raging Bull* was modelled on the *Psycho* shower scene (Wilson, 2011, p.96-97). As La Motta allows himself to be pummelled, the impact of the rapidly edited close-ups, oddly framed high angle shots, and fragmented body parts echoes Hitchcock's most celebrated sequence.

Cape Fear has its own (overblown) *Psycho* moment when Cady disguises himself as murdered maid Graciella, who is initially more a mother figure to Danielle than Leigh. However, this contribution came not from Scorsese, but Steven Spielberg, who suggested it in a script session with Wesley Strick (interview with author). Spielberg also suggested the scene where Cady 'ruins' a family trip to see *Problem Child* (Dugan, 1990) (interview with author). This seems to have been a holdover from a scene Spielberg wanted for *Jaws*, in which Quint would howl through a showing of *Moby Dick* (Huston, 1956) until he was the only audience member remaining. The idea had to be abandoned after the rights holder to *Moby Dick* requested Spielberg not feature the film in that way

– said rights holder was original Sam Bowden, Gregory Peck (Bouzereau, 1995). That Peck named the production company behind 1962's *Cape Fear* Melville Productions provides an indication of his regard for that fishy tale. Coincidentally, *Moby Dick* would go on to inspire Scorsese on *Taxi Driver*, in which he used that film's style of colour printing to desaturate the bloody climax in his movie, thereby avoiding an 'X' rating in the US (*Taxi Driver* audio commentary). The film was certified 'X' in the UK, where the classification did not carry the same association with hardcore pornography.

"Hitchcock is always on my mind," Scorsese is quoted as saying. "If the original (*Cape Fear*) had been directed by Hitchcock, I'd never have touched it" (Wilson, 2011, p.169; 292). It's easy to see why the Catholic Hitchcock landed such an impression; their anxieties and thematic preoccupations overlap, and Scorsese's dynamic style echoes Hitchcock's directorial stamp. Both adopt subjective presentations of reality, externalising characters' emotional and mental states. Often called the most personal of directors, Scorsese frequently places the audience in his position: "I *do* want them to see the way I see" (Thompson/Christie, 1996, p.88).

Visual influence is also found in the work of Val Lewton, Roger Corman and Mario Bava. What Scorsese calls Bava's "Italian Gothic" (Thompson/Christie, 1996, p.103), with its heavy coloured-gel lighting, attention to atmosphere, and lurid displays of violence, is echoed in *Cape Fear*. On the DVD audio commentary for *Taxi Driver*, a film indebted to horror cinema, the director notes: "The camera moves for Travis' paranoia are in direct line with the tradition of the horror film. The camera moves by Mario Bava in the Italian films of the sixties to Mark Robson in *Isle of the Dead* to Jacques Tourneur in *Cat People*, any of the Val Lewton pictures. Not that you sit down and say, 'Hey, let's do the moves from a horror film.' But, somehow from my subconscious they're interpreted that way on paper. It has the same kind of dread that I was hoping to communicate to the audience."

This drawing on horror cinema is evident in the film's climax. Travis Bickle annihilates mafioso and pimps with the relentlessness of James Arness' alien in another Scorsese favourite, *The Thing From Another World* (Nyby, 1951), all given the explosive touch of John Carpenter's 1982 remake, courtesy of prosthetics supplied by *The Exorcist*'s make-up artist Dick Smith. While *Mean Streets*' climax frenetically depicts De Niro's Johnny

Boy sustaining a gushing gunshot wound to the neck, *Taxi Driver*'s carnage is more in line with the violence in Scorsese's 1967 short, *The Big Shave*. In both the camera observes with a cool detachment, the director understanding that the graphic make-up effects need little stylistic embellishment.

The Big Shave features an object favoured in horror cinema, an object Scorsese has fetishised most during his career: the mirror. In *The Passion of Martin Scorsese*, Annette Wernblad argues for Scorsese's filmography being a cinema of the Jungian shadow: the suppressed aspect of ourselves that permits us to operate within society, but if totally buried can fester and erupt in psychologically and physically painful ways (2011, p.6). A mirror is the most elegant visual method of conveying this idea. In the "You talkin' to me?" scene, Travis Bickle's madness is literally reflected back at him. *Raging Bull* opens and closes with Jake La Motta confronting his bloated self in the mirror, taking his fallen reflection to task through the "I coulda been a contender" speech from *On the Waterfront* (Kazan, 1954). After Paul has bailed on Marcy in *After Hours*, his guilt comically manifests in graffiti of a man's penis being bitten by a shark, drawn next to a toilet mirror. The shadow self can also reside in another character: Johnny Boy for Charlie in *Mean Streets*, Rupert Pupkin for Jerry Langford in *The King of Comedy*, Judas for Jesus in *The Last Temptation of Christ*. In the next chapter we will discuss how this reaches an apotheosis in *Cape Fear*.

Appropriately, mirrors loom large in Scorsese's first unmistakable venture into horror territory. In 1986, Steven Spielberg invited him to direct an episode of the short-lived TV series *Amazing Stories* (1986). Penned by *After Hours* scribe Joe Minion from a story by Spielberg, *Mirror, Mirror* tells the tale of horror writer Jordan Manmouth (Sam Waterston), who begins to see a mysterious cloaked phantom (Tim Robbins, unrecognisable) bearing down upon him whenever he looks into a mirror. Or, as it transpires, any reflective surface. Echoing *After Hours*' fear of women, the killing stroke arrives when Manmouth comes face-to-face with the phantom in the reflection of his lover's eye. Manmouth then becomes the phantom in the real world, and chooses to kill himself rather than live as this dark reflection. *Mirror, Mirror* evokes the atmosphere of classic horror, quoting Hammer Studios in a clip from *The Plague of the Zombies* (Gilling, 1966) and referencing the Italian chillers of Mario Bava and Dario Argento. The shot of Manmouth's chauffeur's eyes reflected in the rearview mirror is a direct quote from *Taxi*

Driver, linking the urban horror of that movie with the fantastical chills of this foray into TV.

Manmouth's lover is named Karen, played by Helen Shaver, who had previously worked with Scorsese on *The Color of Money* (1986). Coincidentally, Karen was Leigh's name in Wesley Strick's early drafts of *Cape Fear*, but was changed because Henry Hill's wife in *Goodfellas* was also named Karen, and Scorsese was tired of hearing that name yelled over and over for months (interview with author). In my discussion with him, Strick did not recall the change to Leigh being a reference to *Psycho*'s Janet Leigh. Yet, this would have surely struck Scorsese, particularly as Jessica Lange's hair styling echoes Leigh's in the Hitchcock film.

Endings to Scorsese films can carry the sting of a horror climax. The granddaddy of these is *Taxi Driver*. Travis Bickle's closing flash of mania, startled by his own reflection (naturally) in the rearview mirror, is a Palme d'Or winning film's equivalent to Freddy Krueger popping up for one last fright. Assisting the impact of this moment is the jarring pop of a reversed cymbal crash, a suggestion from Bernard Herrmann. A vanquished monster returning stronger than ever occurs in *The King of Comedy*, with Rupert Pupkin out of prison and a celebrity in the same ironic fashion as Travis Bickle. Tommy De Vito returns from the dead to figuratively shoot Henry Hill (and the audience) at the end of *Goodfellas*, combining the gangster movie, the horror film, and the Western, as the shot directly quotes Edwin S. Porter's *The First Great Train Robbery* (1903).

SCORSESE AS VIRGIL IN THE INFERNO

The Last Temptation of Christ's shrill angelic choir accompanying Jesus' acceptance of his divinity closes the film on a jump scare. Scorsese's literal passion project trades in horror imagery: the raising of Lazarus is depicted as a terrifying act, complete with a jolt as the resurrected man's gnarled hand bursts into frame. Make-up here is more reminiscent of a Lucio Fulci zombie flick than a Cecil B. DeMille biblical epic.

Scorsese has said his life is movies and religion. Often it is *horror* movies and religion. Not many filmmakers would mention Mario Bava's *Kill, Baby… Kill* (1966) when discussing *The Last Temptation of Christ* (Thompson/Christie, 1996, p.143). Not that religion automatically equates to horror, but horror cinema often draws inspiration from religious themes. By articulating its religious subject matter with cutting edge FX and William Friedkin's near-documentary directing style, Scorsese favourite *The Exorcist* revolutionised the genre. The film also offered something absent in most Scorsese movies no matter how deep their religious themes: the possibility of redemption. In *Martin Scorsese's Divine Comedy*, Catherine O'Brien calls the director's cinema "Dantesque", showing "visions of (a Living) Hell; a (Daily) Purgatory and a striving for Paradise" (2018, p.5). Whether Paradise is ever a possibility for Scorsese characters is debatable. They seem largely trapped in the Inferno, sometimes reaching Purgatorio, but with Paradisio out of reach.

That the promise of damnation is so prevalent in Scorsese's cinema may have to do with an active imagination raised in a Catholic upbringing. More precisely, the pre-Vatican II Catholic church, before some of the more restrictive and punitive elements were softened or removed. As fellow Catholic Roger Ebert recalled, "…we were drilled on mortal sins, venial sins, sanctifying grace, the fires of hell…" (Ebert, 2008, p.1). The possibility of damnation and the concept of salvation impacted the young Scorsese, to the point where he considered entering the priesthood (Thompson/Christie, 1996, p.12). Women and rock n' roll are reasons given for why his vocation did not stick, but the prosaic explanation that his grades and attendance record fell short is a more likely answer. Even so, women and rock n' roll would go on to preoccupy both him and his films. Beyond the tenets of Catholicism, religion in Scorsese's early life was often inflected with a Gothic-tinged mortal dread. During the Cold War, he and his classmates would be rushed into the catacombs of St. Patrick's Old Cathedral for drills in case of a nuclear strike. "The camera movement in a lot of my films certainly comes from creeping around those catacombs, with the sound effects of the echoing rosary" (quoted in O'Brien, 2018, p.34).

As in many of the eleven horror films on his list, Scorsese's cinema is preoccupied with reconciling the spiritual with the corporeal, particularly when linked to sexuality, which the filmmaker has said he correlates with the "reptilian, shameful, ignoble" due to his Catholicism, adding that, "Some of us never manage to free ourselves from that guilt" (Wilson, 2011, p.154-155). Sex, guilt and punishment are present from the beginning of his career. *Who's That Knocking at My Door* climaxes with a montage of statues in states of violent martyrdom, while lead character J.R. attempts to confess a sexual relationship with a character credited only as 'The Girl' (Zoe Bethune). That film also features a Madonna/whore complex that would resurface in many of the director's films. Women are idealised, cast as saints until, in the men's eyes, they are sullied by life, experience or desire. They are then cast aside or must themselves be redeemed by men looking for salvation.

Chapter 3 discusses the depiction of women in Scorsese's films, including *Who's That Knocking at My Door*'s confused rape subplot, and the impact of religion. For now, it is worth noting that Scorsese's cinema critiques the male viewpoint as immature and destructive, but the guilt-inducing shadow of religion repeatedly hangs over scenes of intimacy. Scorsese has also shown himself to be simply more interested in the male characters. 'The Girl' has the most dramatic and challenging arc, but she is adjunct to the director's interest in J.R.'s emotional and spiritual turmoil. This narrative device is reused by the filmmaker in other films, including *Cape Fear*.

Alongside this is the director's attraction to unsympathetic characters. While never condoning their actions, he searches for the humanity within them. A Christian pursuit, invoking Matthew 7:1 – "Judge not, that ye be not judged" – this has created impressive examinations of male fragility and destructive machismo, as seen in *Taxi Driver*, *Raging Bull*, *The King of Comedy*, *Goodfellas*, and others. Yet, in *Cape Fear*, a tension arises: Max Cady is a serial rapist targeting the wife and child of a flawed 'hero'. The film is careful not to create pity for Cady, but searching for humanity in such a monster, particularly within a film dressed in the production values and style of a Hollywood A-picture, may be one reason accusations of misogyny were levelled against it.

When reviewing the Catholic influence within Scorsese films, their visual creation of hellish environments is the aspect most immediately noticeable. This convention was present from the beginning: the 1959 short film *Vesuvius VI*, a "miniature epic set in Ancient Rome," ended with the credit "Directed by Martin Scorsese" being engulfed in flame (Thompson/Christie, 1996, p.13). Fire and smoke appear with infernal connotations throughout his work. During Jesus' forty days and nights in the desert in *The Last Temptation of Christ*, Satan appears as a large, majestic flame. In *Mean Streets*, Charlie (Harvey Keitel) habitually punishes himself with fire, holding his fingers over a burning match or the flame from a stove in a restaurant kitchen. That restaurant is about to be given to Charlie by his mobster uncle, taken from an owner who cannot meet loan repayments.

For characters in Scorsese's films, life and religion is all about what is owed upwards. Charlie's thoughts are dominated by the guilt and dread of punishment for accumulated sin. "It's all bullshit except the pain," he says. "The pain of hell. The burn from a lighted match increased a million times" (Scorsese, 1973). Charlie goes on to say Hell holds two forms of pain, the physical and spiritual – spiritual being the worst, that of eternal damnation. Similarly, *Raging Bull* sees Jake La Motta begging for water as he sizzles in a sauna preparing for an upcoming fight, but also a taste of the punishment that awaits once his actions cause him to lose everything.

Goodfellas' Henry Hill (Ray Liotta) and Tommy De Vito (Joe Pesci) are themselves the destroyers of Eden, corrupting everything and everyone around them. Scorsese wryly invokes this when they bankrupt and torch The Bamboo Lounge, a club decorated in the style of an island paradise. Eden has been well and truly tapped dry, it seems. Earlier in the movie, the teenage Henry sells his soul to the Mafia by committing arson in a used car lot. Fleeing the scene of the crime, the film freeze-frames him against a backdrop of fire as the cars explode. In 1985's *After Hours*, Paul smokes a joint lit from the large flame of a candle in Marcy's red-walled bedroom. Marcy is the temptation he has followed down into SoHo, a decision that will transform his world into a comically threatening Hades. Another character residing in a hell of his own making is De Niro's deluded, dangerous Rupert Pupkin in *The King of Comedy*. Dwelling in his mother's (red) basement, acting out fantasies of being a chat show host, Pupkin is a deceiver of everyone around him, including himself. An ambiguous ending leaves the audience to decide whether the self-deception continues, or if he has achieved the ironic salvation of celebrity success.

In Scorsese movies, red colour schemes denote Hell, damnation and danger. The bar Charlie frequents in *Mean Streets* is lit so scarlet it resembles a photographer's dark room. The hangout is a cave of temptation and perdition, where topless dancers perform on stage while in the men's room customers shoot heroin or each other. Small wonder the bar is underground. Also subterranean is Henry Hill's path into the

Copacabana nightclub, with girlfriend Karen (Lorraine Bracco) on his arm. Sidestepping the long queue, Henry leads his wide-eyed date through a suitably red-walled service tunnel, past a bouncer eating a large sandwich (gluttony) and two staff members making out (lust, sloth), whom Henry jokingly berates with "Every time, every time you two! Don't you work?"

An infernal red is omnipresent in *Goodfellas*. It washes over the entire screen as Henry Hill recalls the murder of a mob boss in the trunk of his car. The tablecloths in the Copacabana are red when Bobby Vinton sends Henry and Karen champagne, tempting her to step further into Henry's life. When Tommy berates Henry for laughing too hard at his jokes, the Bamboo Lounge is lit red, and a sense of danger is reinforced by certain diners wearing complementary red costumes. Scorsese acknowledges this infernal influence when describing *Wiseguy: Life in a Mafia Family*, Nick Pileggi's 1985 source book: "It seemed that Nick was taking us through the different levels of purgatory and hell in the underworld, like Virgil or like Dante" (O'Brien, 2018, p.5). This all may look like Paradise, but one wrong word can put you directly in the Inferno.

Sticking with the Inferno, New York of the 1970s was fertile ground for Scorsese and screenwriter (and Calvinist) Paul Schrader to depict Hell on Earth. From *Taxi Driver*'s opening credits the audience knows it is travelling through an underworld. Travis Bickle's yellow taxicab emerges from, and plunges into, thick steam rising from the streets. Red light washes over his eyes as he surveys the city by night, rendered an abstract landscape of unsettling shapes through the rain slicked windscreen. Steam engulfs passers-by, the billows coloured crimson as the director's credit appears. That steam will roll over the ring in *Raging Bull*, and shroud Paul's journey through the night in *After Hours*. That red wash will accompany Scorsese's credit at the beginning of *Cape Fear*, over a shot of a tear drop, or a drop of blood, or a bloody tear…

Does the presence of a higher power temper any of this mortal dread? Rarely. Scorsese's characters search for salvation and are typically still searching, or have accepted purgatory, come the closing credits. A loving God is absent, characters best described by Travis Bickle's self-applied label: "I am God's lonely man." Yet the director frequently employs high angle shots, sometimes referred to as 'God shots' or 'God's-eye-view shots.' Scorsese calls them "the priest's-eye-view", reflecting the viewpoint looking down at the implements of Mass set upon the altar (Ebert, 2008, p.275). To less-religious audiences, the more general 'God's-eye-view' is a better description. These visuals seem to be observing events from a higher vantage point (the overhead tracking shot regarding *Taxi Driver*'s climactic carnage), or sitting in judgement (Paul Newman's Fast Eddie realising pride has led to him being hustled in *The Color of Money*, Tommy De Vito dropping to the floor after being executed in *Goodfellas*). Scorsese's own interpretation of these shots, however, lends an even bleaker view. If they are merely replicating the priest's view of the altar, then God truly is absent, even in the overhead shot of Jesus' journey to Calvary in *The Last Temptation of Christ*. It is a notion the director would wrestle onto the screen, and then wrestle with, in *Silence*.

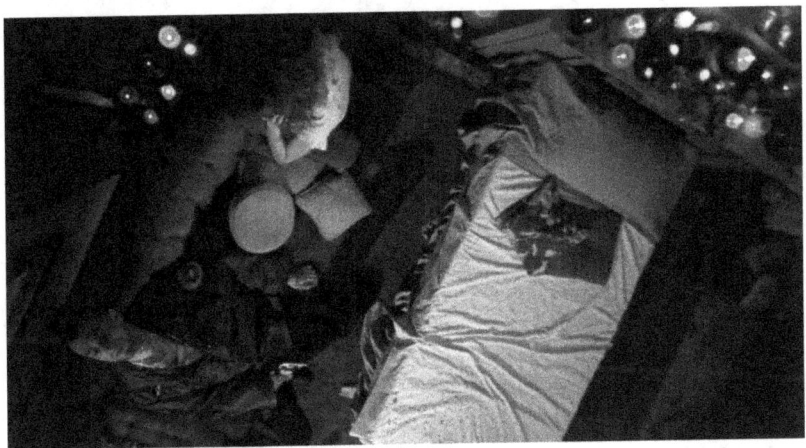

Fig. 5 A God's eye view at the end of Taxi Driver © Columbia Pictures

This notion brings us back to classic horror fiction. In *Taxi Driver*, *After Hours*, *Cape Fear*, and later *Bringing out the Dead*, *Shutter Island* (2010) and *Silence*, there is a near cosmic dread that comes with the thought of being alone in the universe. Rather than scripture, these characters seemingly live by H.P. Lovecraft's philosophy, "The oldest and strongest emotion of mankind is fear, and the oldest and strongest kind of fear is fear of the unknown" (Lovecraft, 1927). Which could explain why violence in Scorsese films is scrappy and messy, but for the characters is at times almost ecstatic. Charlie holding his hand to the fire demonstrates a desire to reach God. Travis Bickle's culmination of his mission is a massacre that baptises him in blood. Max Cady believes violent suffering will bring about Sam Bowden's salvation from a higher power.

In *The Big Shave*, sacrifice and martyrdom are depicted with a minimalist elegance reminiscent of fellow Catholic director Robert Bresson. *The Big Shave* was Scorsese's first colour film. It had to be. This six-minute non-narrative piece dispassionately regards an unnamed man (Peter Bernuth) repeatedly shaving himself, registering no emotion as he begins mutilating his face. Monochrome photography would have blunted the impact of deep-red blood contrasted against a gleaming white bathroom. The short film establishes a template for the psychosis that often dwells in the Scorsese male. As Annette Wernblad notes, "…there is a fine line between trying to get redemption through self-flagellation and complete psychosis, [leaving] us wondering which side of the mirror this particular man is on" (2011, p.80).

Likewise, *Mean Street*'s Charlie, *Taxi Driver*'s Travis Bickle, *New York, New York*'s (1977) Jimmy Doyle, and *Raging Bull*'s Jake La Motta. These men seek out pain in life, and when they cannot find it they create it to ensure their suffering. *Raging Bull* exemplifies this. While not a boxing fan, for research Scorsese attended two fights at Madison Square Garden. He took from them the blood-soaked sponge washing the boxer's chest and blood dripping off the ropes (Thompson/Christie, 1996, p.80). Both these moments made it into the finished film, as La Motta sacrifices himself to rival Sugar Ray Robinson, penance for beating both his wife and brother while in a jealous rage. The blows are depicted in rapid edits, but the visuals slow so the audience can register blood spraying from cuts above La Motta's eye and forehead. Blood splashes onto ringside commentators, underlining the impression of a biblical execution. Jake absorbs the punishment not for all humankind, but solely for himself, for the sins he has committed. In the complicated world of a Scorsese movie, La Motta will fall from grace again and his penance will not be as swift, continuing beyond the film's fade-out. Again, the worst pain is the spiritual.

While Scorsese would not carry the gore of *Taxi Driver* or *Raging Bull* over to his staging of the crucifixion in *The Last Temptation of Christ*, he did look to his B-movie beginnings, borrowing shots from the climactic crucifixion in *Boxcar Bertha*. When discussing *Taxi Driver* with the director, Scorsese's parish priest, Rev. Francis Principe, said, "I'm glad you ended it on Easter Sunday and not on Good Friday." (Reidy, 2012). While this arguably misunderstands the film's climactic sting, it is an effective way to summarise the director's work. To the point where the quote has been bastardised as "Too much Good Friday, not enough Easter Sunday," when discussing his output (Reidy, 2012).

Cape Fear is all Good Friday. Sam assuming himself as an ultimate arbiter of the law is not regarded favourably by higher powers suggested to be at play. To dramatise this, Scorsese supercharges the foreboding religion-inspired themes and images of his earlier work, transforming a standard revenge thriller into a blood and thunder horror film.

CHAPTER 2: DEVIL IN THE DETAILS – HORROR AND *CAPE FEAR*

Michael Henry Wilson calls Scorsese's *Cape Fear*, "…the first of his films that belongs to a clearly defined genre, in this case the thriller" (2011, p.305). But as we shall explore in this chapter, like the swampy waters of the film's river its genre is anything but clear.

When reading critical commentary on *Cape Fear* it is notable how many writers invoke the horror genre. Equally important is how horror is used as evidence that *Cape Fear* saw Scorsese slumming it. Lesley Stern in *The Scorsese Connection* comments, "The operatic in *Cape Fear*… brings together a yearning for the sublime with an invincibly bathetic craving for B-grade Horror" (1995, p.170). A similar sentiment is offered by Pam Cook in her *Sight and Sound* article, 'Scorsese's Masquerade': "It's no secret that, in a bid for commercial success, Scorsese decided to remake J. Lee Thompson's taut black and white thriller as a horror movie… *Cape Fear* owes everything to low-budget horror movies – Abel Ferrara's 1987 [sic] *Ms. 45 (Angel of Vengeance)* for instance" (1992, p.14).

In Chapter 1, we reviewed horror's influence on Scorsese's movies up to *Cape Fear*. Arguments have been made that he is a frequent traveller through the genre. In *Nightmare Movies* Kim Newman writes, "The poet laureate of the psycho movie is Martin Scorsese, whose horror films are rarely recognised as such" (2011, p.134).

In *Cape Fear*, Leigh recalls her husband's time as a defence lawyer with the softly caustic remark, "Oh, I remember those days; ol' Slippery Sam." Horror can be similarly difficult to get hold of and hang on to. Opinions inevitably shift over time, so what was once regarded as terrifying now seems cosy. 1931's *Frankenstein* and 1954's *The Creature from the Black Lagoon* (Arnold) are unlikely to frighten today's horror audience, for whom the biggest shock may be the lack of colour. As its style and conventions continue to be absorbed into other genres, titles once agreed upon as 'horror' are now being reevaluated. With police procedurals on the big screen and small routinely tackling darker subject matter, often with graphic make-up prosthetics, film discussion boards and Twitter threads will ask, "Is *The Silence of the Lambs* a horror film?" The same has been asked of *Seven*. An interesting inversion of this can be applied to films such as *Jaws* and *Blue Velvet* (Lynch, 1986), arguing they are horror, not adventure or arthouse-thriller, respectively.

Even the commonly understood principle aims of horror – to shock, scare, repulse – have been lifted and shifted into unlikely environments. *24* (2001-14), *Daredevil* (2015-18) and *Jessica Jones* (2015-19) use horror conventions to elicit these responses in TV series still best read as belonging to thriller and superhero categories. Brigid Cherry succinctly captures the difficulty in offering one simple definition of horror. She argues that the genre's longevity, coupled with its drawing upon myriad sources such as novels, theatre, real life, etc. from different countries, means it is most usefully viewed as a diverse group of sub-genres (2009, p.4).

Cherry lists these sub-genres as:

- The Gothic
- Supernatural, occult and ghost film
- Psychological horror
- Monster movies
- Slashers
- Body horror, splatter and gore films
- Exploitation cinema, video nasties or other forms of explicitly violent films

    (Cherry, 2009. p.5-6).

Bar 'monster movies', we will see elements of *Cape Fear* in all these groupings, which will be no surprise to those familiar with Scorsese's back catalogue. Renowned for his cine-literacy, when working in a new genre (the thriller), and uncertain of his ability to be successful within it, it is no surprise that he focussed on those aforementioned "powerful sensations". Even less surprising that he looked to horror cinema to achieve them.

When cameras started rolling on 1991's *Cape Fear*, horror cinema had enjoyed almost twenty years of mainstream commercial and cultural success. *The Exorcist*, with its demon child plot, had entered the pop culture lexicon and spawned a slew of religious themed shockers. *The Omen* (Donner, 1976), starring Gregory Peck, was a similarly influential box office hit. Whether *Deliverance* is a horror film is up for debate, but its success popularised a rural or 'backwoods' horror sub-genre typified by *The Texas Chain*

Saw Massacre (Hooper, 1974) (whose title is seen on a cinema marquee in urban-horror film *Taxi Driver*), *The Hills Have Eyes* (Craven, 1977) and *Rituals* (Carter, 1977). Both *The Exorcist* and *Deliverance* have antecedents in horror films from previous decades. 'Backwoods horror' was a trend supercharged by the arrival of *Psycho* and given violent, censor-rebuking make-overs during the 1960s by such films as *Two Thousand Maniacs* (Lewis, 1964) and *Spider Baby* (Hill, 1967). Old Nick too had hits in the swinging sixties, with Hammer's *The Devil Rides Out* (Fisher, 1968) and *Rosemary's Baby* (Polanski, 1968). Like *Rosemary's Baby*, differentiating *Deliverance* and *The Exorcist* from other horror movies was the kind of box-office receipts that only come with crossover audience success.

Devil horror and rural horror are felt in the sub-genre that would dominate horror cinema in the 1980s: the slasher movie. Prototypes of the slasher include *A Bay of Blood* (Bava, 1971), a key influence on the first two *Friday the 13th* instalments, and *Black Christmas* (Clark, 1974). As well as cementing conventions of the colour *giallo*, Mario Bava's *Blood and Black Lace* (1964) can also be viewed as a proto-slasher. Generating too many titles to mention here, the slasher cycle proper was launched with the unexpected success of John Carpenter's *Halloween* (1978). It would be dominated by that movie's subsequent franchising, plus the long running series of both *Friday the 13th* (1980-2003) and *A Nightmare on Elm Street* (1984-2003). These movies remained profitable throughout the 1980s and crossed into the mainstream, particularly *Elm Street*.

Detractors accused slashers of relying on spectacular gore and nubile flesh to compensate for lazy plots and thin characterisation, tarnishing horror anew with the routinely applied no-brow label. An argument can be made that the term 'psychological thriller' was created to allow cinemagoers intellectual peace of mind when opting to watch a fright film. But, devil horror, rural horror and the slasher shaped and evolved the genre to the point where conventions and expectations would seep into other movies, regardless of intent. In my conversation with Wesley Strick, he said Southern inhospitality movies and slasher films were not front of mind when writing *Cape Fear*. The film's most graphic moment of violence – Cady mutilating Lori's face – came from of De Niro's research and was not, in Strick's words, "just a nod to the slasher genre". Yet, these three branches of horror can be seen in *Cape Fear*, dramatised through that most terrifying of horror staples: the family.

Home is Where the Hurt is

> The family is the best microcosm to work with. If you go much beyond that you're getting away from a lot of the roots of our own primeval feelings. Let's face it, most of the basic stories and the basic feelings involve very few people: Mommy, Daddy, me, siblings, and the few other people in the room. – Wes Craven (quoted in Wood, 2003, p.114)

Eight of the eleven films Scorsese lists as the scariest of all time focus on familial trauma, guilt and betrayal (*Isle of the Dead*, *Dead of Night* and *Night of the Demon* are the – arguable - exceptions). In Scorsese's cinema, the family can be a repository of intimidation or violent recrimination, e.g. *Mean Streets*, *New York, New York*, *Raging Bull*, and *Goodfellas*. Annette Wernblad posits the intriguing suggestion that Rupert Pupkin's seen-but-not-heard nagging mum (voiced by Scorsese's actual mother, Catherine) has actually passed and is a *Psycho*-style figment of his imagination (2011, p.94). Travis Bickle's anniversary-*cum*-birthday card to his parents also carries a suspicion this is correspondence to the departed. Appropriate, then, that Scorsese has proven such a talented chronicler of the Mafia, the ultimate example of a family that never gives, only takes. Or that he would make a mob movie titled *The Departed* (2006). Even when the family is absent, a proxy family of friends and acquaintances offers scant more support. In *The Color of Money*, Vincent is betrayed by surrogate father Eddie. Paul in *After Hours* is a bad boyfriend, while the female characters are threatening wife and/or mother figures. Even Jesus struggles with a distant father.

Cape Fear remains the director's bleakest depiction of a family because it is both terrorised by and inadvertent creator of the monstrous Cady. Scorsese frames his antagonist as "…an evil spirit who represents the fear and guilt of each member of the family… The family is vulnerable from the start because it is dysfunctional. Like every family I know! These Bowdens are all imperfect, so I'm able to love them!" (Wilson, 2011, p.170).

This notion of the family generating its own torment was a key element of horror's evolution in the 1970s, and *Cape Fear*'s depiction of the family has roots in the shifting values of that decade. As the above-mentioned three horror sub-genres began dominating cultural conversation, the call was increasingly coming from inside the house.

Fig. 6 Marital discord in Cape Fear

Andrew Tudor identifies two trends in the genre, Secure Horror and Paranoid Horror, and both are useful when analysing *Cape Fear*, particularly in its relation to the 1962 original. Secure Horror, which Tudor ascribes to movies pre-1960s (i.e. before *Psycho*), sees the threat as typically external to the norm. Protagonists have an expertise that allows them to defeat the menace, while authorities and the established order are essentially just and worth preserving. Social agencies create boundaries that separate the protagonist from the destructive antagonist, preserving societal norms, exemplified by the nuclear family. Come the film's close, normality is restored (1989, p.103).

While I do not view 1962's *Cape Fear* as a horror film, Tudor's definition of Secure Horror largely applies. Wesley Strick stuck close to changes screenwriter James R. Webb made to MacDonald's book for the original movie; basic plot events are so similar that the opening credits state the 1991 film is based on both MacDonald's novel and Webb's script. But, Strick abandons the endorsement of frontier justice found in both *The Executioners* and the first movie. In Thompson's film Cady is depicted as antithetical to the values espoused by the Bowdens. As in the novel, the morally upstanding Sam of the earlier version tackled Cady while he was raping a young girl, and subsequently testified at his trial. Therefore, when the law is ineffective in containing the ex-con, Sam's planned vigilantism receives tacit legal approval by the presence of an Officer Kersek to assist him in killing Cady. Interestingly, this first adaptation is the only version to date in which Cady survives; the Hays Code would not have permitted an endorsement of lethal vigilantism, and it would have sat uneasy with the real-life politics of famed Hollywood liberal Gregory Peck. But, as per the rape-revenge narrative, Sam twists the law to accommodate his vengeance, implying that Cady's imprisonment is a slower form of execution, "…until the day you *rot*." Crucially, the Bowden family is united in their fight against the psychotic ex-con. This unity is taken even further in the novel, both in the gung-ho bloodlust of Sam's wife Carol and when the family enjoy a day of group gun practice; preparation in case Cady comes calling.

With Paranoid Horror, protagonists are overwhelmed by the encroaching peril and any intervention to stop it usually fails. Institutions prove unreliable and unable to maintain harmony. Chaos and disorder are the norms as victims form their own defences against the threat, one that is often internal as boundaries grow diffuse, and is routinely undefeated come the unresolved ending. Scorsese's *Cape Fear* fits snugly into this bracket. Sam's ethical failing in suppressing evidence at Cady's trial marks both the system weakening and the conception point of Max Cady the avenger. Coupled with Sam's later infidelity, this creates flaws in the Bowdens' defences, while rendering unworkable an endorsement of vigilante justice. With Sam being Cady's lawyer rather than a witness for the prosecution, the remake is thus transformed into a narrative about the dangers of vigilante action, that violent example of excessive pride. Sam rejects the supremacy of law, thereby undermining the foundations he believes hold him and his family safe. Subsequent attempts to double down on this impulse (hiring goons to assault Cady, enticing the ex-con to break into his house) are shown to be just as damaging to himself and those around him.

In an example of blanket auteurism, this change to Sam's role in the story is often ascribed to Scorsese. In fact, it was a plot switch Strick added from draft one, explaining to me: "I think it's something any half decent screenwriter would have done in updating the material… I liked the irony of it. In a macro sense Sam did the right thing, but we can't condone that kind of behaviour, especially in a professional context. It wasn't necessarily immoral, but it was unethical, and he pays a huge price for it" (interview with author).

Crossing boundaries becomes a recurring motif in the film. Cady taunts the Bowdens by sitting on the wall that bounds their property, a legal act of intimidation and a near-trespass in response to Sam's previous 'trespasses'. Moreover, he gains access to the Bowdens' spacious house early in the film to poison Ben, the family dog. Cady continues to invade their domestic space for the remainder of *Cape Fear*, even when the family relocates to the moving target of the houseboat. This near paranormal slipperiness is encapsulated in Sam's escalating panic when he says to Kersek, "I believe he's able to slip into the house and out undetected. Although is he out, I can't tell. He's either out or he's in, I'm not sure." Kersek, who in this telling is a private investigator Cady suggests was kicked off the force for past misdeeds, replies, "Well, I can't see through walls, Mr. Bowden." This dooms the P.I. because Cady *can*… Sam's transgression has created a force of vengeance the established order cannot withstand. Cady is also able to cross the most important boundary, getting into the heads of the respective Bowdens, either directly with Danielle or indirectly with Leigh. His attack on Lori sows fresh suspicions of adultery. As Sam's dark reflection, Cady can second guess the lawyer's every move, including his final act escape plan. As the Bowdens flee for the houseboat, they drive past a handmade sign reading, 'Where will you spend eternity?', written in lettering markedly similar to Cady's tattoos.

Robert Mitchum's Lt. Elgart compromises societal law by suggesting Sam adopt a vigilante strategy. To this Sam damns the central plan of the original movie when he exclaims, "What are you suggesting, Lieutenant? That I use my family as bait? And then what? I'm going to hope that this psychopath attacks my wife and child? And then what, blow his head off?" Even as the power of the law seems to abandon Sam, it bolsters Cady, who has mastered it while incarcerated. A character feature of the original film, in the 1991 version this self-improvement receives greater emphasis, culminating in Cady's 'trial' of Sam Bowden. Expertise is ineffectual when the antagonist is as skilled as the protagonist.

Robin Wood's *Hollywood from Vietnam to Reagan* is also valuable for identifying in *Cape Fear* elements that began to surface in 1970s American horror. Discussing concepts of repression in socio-political and socio-sexual contexts, Wood claimed 1970s horror depicted an eruption of repressed forces and an exploration of societal taboos, while also acknowledging horror can be reactionary as well as revolutionary (an accusation he targets at slasher cinema) (1986, p.70-94). Wood argued that since the 1960s, horror has contained five recurring motifs: a human psychotic as the monster, the revenge of nature, a satanism or possession theme, the terrible child, and cannibalism. These appear in various forms in *Cape Fear* and, as Wood writes, all are drawn together by "the unifying master figure – the Family" (1986, p.83).

On one level a sexual psychotic, Cady is also coded as a Satanic figure who, in a reverse baptism, rises from the swamps of the Cape Fear river, ready to possess and corrupt. He also demonstrates a predilection for cannibalism, both onscreen with Lori and in information Kersek relays to Sam. Danielle's disgust at her parents' failings makes her the terrible child in Cady's plan, until the full extent of his malevolence is revealed. Horror here is internal, a dark force linked to the family, and erupting from within to destroy the host. Apt then that Wesley Strick likened Cady hanging on to the underside of the Bowden's Cherokee to the facehugger from *Alien* (Scott, 1979) (Bouzereau, 2001). The screenwriter also believes the family in crisis is what drew Scorsese to the material: "A lot's been written about Marty's Catholicism, about his ideas of blood guilt and expiation of sin and all that, but I think his immediate connection to this material was as a domestic melodrama" (Maslin, 1991, p.14).

In many ways, *Cape Fear* literally brings its horrors home. Over fifty-five minutes (47% of the film's running time bar end credits) is set in the Bowden household or on their houseboat. Cady attacks and rapes Lori in her home, and emerges from a gingerbread house on the school stage to seduce Danielle. While we briefly see Cady's apartment, the suggestion is he haunts every area of the Bowdens' lives and domestic space. Freddie Francis externalises this in his cinematography to reflect the Bowden's panic, and explained "...the atmosphere of the house changes with them – it degrades as the story goes along. The thing starts off bright and sunny and then slowly gets more downbeat..." (Morgan, 1991b). Scorsese visualises this most dramatically in the climax, when the Bowdens' house(boat) is ripped apart and consumed by a swirling vortex. God's-eye-view shots of the boat tossed on the stormy river, complemented by Cady's biblical rantings, suggest a higher power at play, setting the stage for the Bowdens' redemption and Cady's (ambiguous) damnation.

A scene featured in both the novel and the 1962 version, in which Cady tells Sam how upon release he kidnapped and raped his ex-wife, then blackmailed her to stay silent, was also shot for the remake. But the monologue was ultimately cut from the finished film, presumably as it detracts from Cady's relentless focus on Sam as the target for his revenge. In Scorsese's version, there is the suggestion that Cady's ex-wife is Loretta, whose name is tattooed on his arm and above the broken heart on his chest. When Lori asks who she is, he replies, "The love of my life who's no longer with us," implying here an even worse fate has befallen his ex-spouse.

Much of the extensive script revisions went on splintering the family. In a draft dated 'August 31, 1990', approximately three months before cameras first rolled, the Bowdens are written as dysfunctional but more united than in the final film. They are shown walking as a family to the cinema (Strick, 1990, p.4) and there is less friction in the dialogue between Sam and Leigh (or Karen as she is named in this draft). In the film, Leigh's suggestion to Sam they get a gun "in case things get a little exciting", followed by, "we'd probably end up using it on each other" is a substitution for "I'm a little scared, Sam" in this earlier draft (Strick, 1990, p.15).

Strick recalls Scorsese telling him that Jessica Lange, "…told me straight up when she signed on she wasn't satisfied with the role as written, and I promised her she'd have your services to help her find a character that is more layered" (interview with author). The writer would realise that Lange "never wanted to play on the nose. If there was a scene in which Leigh was frustrated, she wanted lines that sounded kittenish or girlish, and then she would play the frustration beneath that" (interview with author). This explains why Leigh is generally more supportive of Danielle in this 'August 31, 1990' draft, and became more sardonic after Lange's involvement in shaping the character. In the film, Leigh finds a maternal bond with Ben the family dog that is missing with her daughter, telling him, "They switched babies on me in the hospital, didn't they?" That line is missing from the earlier draft, and Leigh and Danielle's exchanges are absent a sarcastic undercurrent (Strick, 1990, p.3).

In the finished film, Danielle has a warmer relationship with Graciella, the family's maid, than she does with her mother. The teenager entering the house with Graciella at the beginning of the movie, brightly conversing in broken Spanish, was added later. In that earlier draft Danielle sees the maid through the kitchen window, but their conversation is not heard (Strick, 1990, p.3). Presumably, the film comparing the maid to the dog as another surrogate family member was unintended insensitivity. Both Leigh and Danielle lose these emotional proxies and must support each other come the houseboat climax, something we shall explore in relation to *Cape Fear* and the trope of the Final Girl.

If Cady represents the Bowdens' collective trauma, then responsibility for that trauma lies with Sam. Sam's decision to suppress evidence can be read as the first crack in his moral armour (or his first prideful action) that would lead to marital infidelity and continued flirtation with female colleagues. As Cady says in separate scenes, "You go everywhere you want with whomever. That much freedom could maybe get a fella into trouble, what you think?" and "I'm gonna teach you the meaning of commitment." The Bowdens fit the archetypal horror family coming out of the 1970s into the 1980s, facing a foe that embodies the principles of Paranoid Horror. But, Scorsese adds another twist of the blade that risks alienating audiences: although viewers can understand the family and their problems, some may find it difficult to muster sympathy for them. As Roger Ebert commented in the 1991 *Siskel & Ebert* review: "[Scorsese has] made it very difficult to identify with any of the characters. Everyone in this movie is flawed or dishonest in one way or another, and the message seems to be that evil corrupts everyone who comes into contact with it."

Ebert also dubs the film a "terrifying tragedy", which speaks to Scorsese's possible intentions; the audience will be battered on the stormy waters of high emotion, without a life jacket of likeability. This may be what Pam Cook meant when writing that the film owed everything to low-budget horror movies. Horror films, particularly those unburdened by the need to generate huge box office to show a profit, can explore troubling situations populated by less than sympathetic characters. For fans of these movies this tension is a bonus, offering an alternative to the four-quadrant appeal found in mainstream Hollywood fare. But, *Cape Fear* is mainstream Hollywood fare. Polished, big-budgeted, and, with De Niro and Lange, sporting two Oscar winners in its lead cast. Gregory Peck and Martin Balsam, both of whom appeared in the 1962 original and cameo here, were also previous Academy Award winners. At this point then, it is worth introducing another practical analytical tool: Robin Wood's concept of the "incoherent text".

Wood argued that certain films were interesting because they failed to marshal their viewpoint into a coherent ideology. The resultant incoherence creates a tension that makes these films fascinating in a way not true of more 'successful' examples of the genre. He ascribes this incoherence to multiple factors: the personal, and possibly contradictory, interests of the filmmakers, cultural assumptions of the viewing audience, and the social milieu in which the film was made (Wood, 1986, p.47). Central to Wood's theory, and his understanding of the horror film, is that society is built on repression. Certain films will justify that repression, others will rail against it, often reflecting the wider attitudes of the time. He sees the damage of crises such as the Vietnam war and Watergate on the national psyche as key factors for a number of 'incoherent texts' in 1970s Hollywood (1986, p.49). While authority and institutions were widely challenged, no satisfactory social or economic alternatives were forthcoming. Counterculture options, e.g. communes and shared houses, were regarded with distrust by a frustrated working and middle class. John G. Avildsen's *Joe* (1970) captures these anxieties but is not itself an incoherent text. By the tragic closing moments it is comfortable with its ideology: action before understanding is catastrophic.

Wood cites *Taxi Driver*, along with *Looking for Mr. Goodbar* (Brooks, 1977) and *Cruising* (Friedkin, 1980), as a prime example of the incoherent text. *Taxi Driver*, he writes, is caught between Scorsese's Catholicism, humanism and fascination with Classical Hollywood, and writer Paul Schrader's "quasi-fascism", plus the societal upheaval against which the film was made. As a result, the film cannot decide what it wants from the character of Travis Bickle (1986, p.51). Time seems to have granted more clarity, with *Taxi Driver* an acknowledged masterpiece of urban alienation and contemporary madness. Society's celebration of the clearly insane Bickle has only gained relevancy in an age of warped celebrity worship, even if he could now be regarded as a spiritual grandfather to self-pitying InCels on social media, plus Joaquin Phoenix's character from *Joker* (Phillips, 2019) *and* the subsequent memes.

Like *Taxi Driver*, *Cape Fear* can be read as an incoherent text, and again the primary reason lies in a character portrayed by Robert De Niro. Max Cady is a serial rapist whose revenge plan includes a fifteen-year-old girl, so there is inevitable friction in casting him as an avenging angel sent to recalibrate Sam's moral lens, particularly when Scorsese has loaded so many emotional problems onto the Bowdens. Compounding this is the question of whether the family *deserves* the level of violence, threat and chaos that crashes into their lives. Sam's ethical transgression is understandable: evidence that

Cady's victim was promiscuous could have resulted in a rapist walking free. Judging by Cady's actions in the film, Sam did prevent other women from being attacked while the rapist was incarcerated. But, the film positions Sam's misdeeds as profound enough to warrant incurring such wrath. By breaking his oath to uphold the Sixth Amendment ("… in every criminal prosecution the accused shall have the assistance of counsel for his defence") Sam has placed his own judgement above that of the law, and by extension all higher authority. His inability to operate within the law speaks to an unchecked pride: he did not believe the prosecution could present a case against Cady that would best his defence. But, if Cady *were* successfully prosecuted in that way, it would have resulted in women perhaps being unafraid that victim-blaming would be a legal weapon used against them. Sam's actions created a rot in the legal profession, and rather than work to resolve it, he retreated into corporate law.

A heady ethical conundrum for audiences expecting the commercial movie Scorsese had signed on to make. Therefore, making Sam promiscuous (something for which Cady's victim would have been lambasted) adds a more audience friendly "sin" that the lawyer needs to redress. Not that infidelity is something Scorsese takes lightly. He once said of his divorces, "I am living in sin and I will go to hell because of it" (Ebert, 2008, p.103). That guilt of marital failure and the need to atone hangs heavy in *Cape Fear*. Or in Scorsese's words, "I introduced guilt into this story. I made it Catholic!" (Wilson, 2011, p.170). Max Cady's Pentecostal fundamentalism is therefore revealed as colourful window dressing; this is a film steeped in the worldview of someone raised in pre-Vatican II Catholicism.

Despite its antagonist's religiosity, there is not a single church in *Cape Fear*. Similarly, although Sam is a lawyer, the only time characters appear in a courtroom is when Cady reveals Sam's perversion of the law in embracing vigilante justice. Penance takes its cue from Charlie's opening monologue in *Mean Streets*: "You don't make up for your sins in the church. You do it in the streets. You do it at home. The rest is bullshit and you know it." Resultantly, characters are denied the easy remedy of the frontier justice enacted in *The Executioners* and the 1962 *Cape Fear*. In the original movie, audiences are invited to feel appalled at how Cady is shielded by legal protections: "A man like that doesn't deserve civil rights," says Sam's wife Peggy (Polly Bergen). By 1991, Sam discovers the ease with which he committed his transgression is replicated throughout the legal system, and safeguards he assumed robust begin to crumble; again, Paranoid Horror brings the societal into the personal space.

J. Lee Thompson's *Cape Fear* avoids ideological incoherence by framing Bowden as a paragon of decency, a near dress rehearsal for Peck's performance as Atticus Finch in *To Kill A Mockingbird* (Mulligan, 1962). Unblemished from the start, he has no difficulty in uniting his family against the predatory menace. When seeing wholesomeness threatened by such evil, the film can justify Sam's reactionary tactics. 1962's *Cape Fear* stress tests society's institutions and certifies them sound. MacDonald's book takes this further by stress testing the law and finding it sound *only when useful*. Unwittingly killing Cady when firing a shot that nicks an artery in the ex-con's arm, Sam later regards the body and "…searched through himself for a sense of shame. And found only a sense of savage satisfaction… the neat and careful layers of civilised instincts and behaviour were peeled back to reveal an intense exultation over the death of an enemy" (MacDonald, 1957, p.192). Reflecting on his experiences and how it has reshaped his view of the law, Sam says, "I think I was getting too stuffy. I was idealizing my profession, and leaning on it too heavily. Now I know it's just a tool… use it wisely and it can help you. And when it's of no use to you, you take a course of action that will be of use" (MacDonald, 1957, p.197). Its very title, *The Executioners*, suggests an institutionally approved taking of life despite moral doubts Sam has earlier in the book. But, there is no room for moral reassurance when Cady is a demon summoned by the family's dysfunction.

The Sam at the end of *The Executioners* is the Sam fourteen years before 1991's *Cape Fear* begins; a man who regards his own judgement as superior to the laws upon which his country is built. In Scorsese's version, however, rather than solving a problem, this abrogation of oath lights a slow-fuse bomb that will explode fourteen years later. While commenting on the conservatism baked into the book and original movie, the remake also critiques a vigilante sub-genre legitimised by the success of *Death Wish*, and which flourished during the 1980s. As Strick said at the time, "…between me and Marty it's certainly not going to seem like Charles Bronson… that was my real fear, that it would be like *Death Wish*" (Morgan, 1991c). Embracing a Reaganite 'might-is-right' philosophy, these films presented a world of chaos impervious to legal sanctions. Direct physical force was the only corrective, dispensed by characters with minimum critical reflection. Best illustrating this are Sylvester Stallone's *Cobra* (Cosmatos, 1986), Chuck Norris' *Silent*

Rage (Miller, 1982) and J. Lee Thompson's *10 To Midnight* (1983). In all three films, the male leads portray lawmen frustrated at how the law prevents them from dispensing true justice. *10 To Midnight* includes a line of dialogue reminiscent of Peggy's ideology from the 1962 film, but amped up for the more-is-more 1980s: "The way the law protects these maggots, you'd think they were an endangered species."

Again, however, the incoherent text of 1991's *Cape Fear* wriggles. Sam's ethical permissiveness creates a fundamentalist (i.e. conservative) force of destruction the film does not condone. Yet, the film does sit in judgement of Sam's ethical and moral weakness by visiting Cady upon him and the family. The politics here seem biblical: God *needs* Satan and Judas to transgress to deliver an Ultimate Justice. Later we shall see how this sits neatly with Cady's view of himself and his mission. Within the more prosaic requirements of mainstream storytelling, however, this leads to Tom Shone's observation that, "There is a strain of seamy, insinuating nastiness to *Cape Fear* that in most thrillers is confined to the villain" (2014, p.155).

A controversial scene not featured in that 'August 31, 1990' draft has Leigh, frustrated after unsatisfactory sex with Sam, sitting at a vanity table and reflected in multiple mirrors. In extreme close-up she applies various lipsticks, the film employing gaudy colour dissolves between shots to highlight her frustration and the artificiality of this release. Leigh spots Cady sitting on the wall of their house, framed against a backdrop of similarly artificially coloured fireworks. The implication here is that Leigh has raised Cady, a notion enhanced by the Scorsese mirror(s), which reflect darker projections of the character standing before them. Or, put another way, speak of the Devil… But this further erodes the film's internal logic. Who has brought Cady here and for what reason? A later scene in the police station has Sam looking into a one-way mirror when Cady is undergoing a strip search on the other side, suggesting the ex-con is reflecting the lawyer's sins back at him. That the scene with Leigh is not in the 'August 31, 1990' draft indicates it was a later result of Strick's work with Lange to deepen the character. So is Cady manipulating the characters or being used by them as a tool of revenge for betrayals between husband and wife?

Fig. 7 Leigh's dissatisfaction reflected back at her

One interpretation offsetting the claim that this is a film in which women side with their rapist is that the scene invokes a staple of the Devil movie, namely characters messing with dark forces whose power they do not understand. A discontented Leigh yearning for more in her life can be compared to Regan communicating with Captain Howdy in *The Exorcist*. Both actions unwittingly invite a vampiric entity into their lives that will prey on weakness and division. This comparison does infantilise the adult character, but also shifts Cady further into the realm of the demonic, intensifying the feeling that an unnatural force is manipulating the family. The supernatural layering applied to Max Cady moves the character from serial rapist to a Satanic figure. Tension remains, however, in his use of sexual violence as a primary weapon, even when suggested more than depicted, particularly against a minor, an element of the film more unsettling to audiences now than at time of release.

But, when De Niro said he and Scorsese could "*do* something with this guy", he meant it. In their hands, Max Cady becomes a horror supervillain. A fiend with roots in pulp fiction and film noir, horror cinema and fairy tales, and Gothic and Southern Gothic literature.

MAXIMUM OVERWROUGHT

I spent fourteen years in an eight-by-nine cell, surrounded by people who were less than human. My mission in that time was to become more than human. – Max Cady, *Cape Fear* (1991)

Realising there was potential for Max Cady to cast a shadow long after *Cape Fear*'s release, Robert De Niro dove into the research he regards as crucial to a successful performance. Alongside working with writer Wesley Strick, the actor employed researchers to assemble material from which he could fashion the villain (Strick interview with author). Poring over books on prison life, criminal insanity, serial killers, rape, and revenge, De Niro also reviewed Nietzschean philosophy and Dante. Neo-Freudian Karen Horney's work on neuroses and the craving for recognition and control, plus vengeance refracted through Pentecostal fundamentalism and Messiah complexes were other areas of research that contributed to De Niro shaping the character. The actor also talked to patients in mental institutions and watched tapes of sex offenders describing their crimes. Barbara Kopple's 1976 documentary *Harlan County U.S.A* helped him work on the accent (Levy, 2014, p.380).

Rather than the original *Cape Fear*, the Robert Mitchum film that De Niro looked to was Charles Laughton's 1955 noir-fable *The Night of the Hunter*. But he also found ways into Cady through his own back catalogue, returning to *Taxi Driver* and *Raging Bull*, along with the little remembered 'traumatised Vietnam vet' movie *Jacknife* (Jones, 1989) and *Bang the Drum Slowly* (Hancock, 1973), in which he played a terminally ill low-IQ baseball player (Levy, 2014, p.380). While Strick's script mentioned Cady was tattooed, De Niro decided to develop the idea of the word made flesh, investing money to design the body art that would become Cady's mission statement. The actor's immersive research into both Cady's psychology and physicality suggests he was consciously creating something bigger than life, a force of nature, a notion borne out in his description of the antagonist: "He just keeps coming and coming… He's like the Alien or the Terminator" (Levy, 2014, p.381).

Treating Max Cady as beyond mere human evil is evident in every telling of the *Cape Fear* story. Author John D. MacDonald keeps the character out of Sam Bowden's sight for most of *The Executioners*, making him simultaneously elusive and omnipresent, too big to be contained on the page.

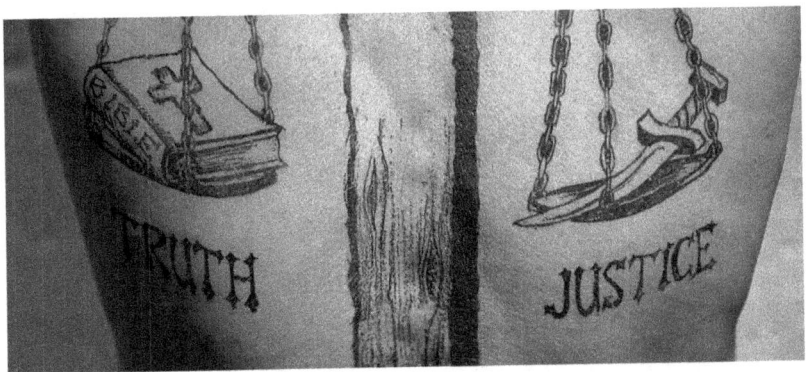

Fig. 8 The word made flesh

Running counter to 1991-Cady's desire to "become more than human", the book and Thompson's screen adaptation liken his larger-than-life presence to the animalistic. MacDonald's first description of his antagonist conjures up an image of the missing link between human and primate: "Dark hair grew low on his forehead. Heavy mouth and jaw. Small brown eyes set in deep and simian sockets" (MacDonald, 1957, p.6). Though this does not describe Robert Mitchum's Cady, the 1962 movie keeps the analogy through dialogue. A private investigator tells Sam, "A type like that is an animal. So you've gotta fight him like an animal."

Rather than being ape-like, Mitchum's villain is a snake, the actor's sneering grin never meeting his dark cobra eyes. This is best illustrated during the climax, as Cady glides through the swampy undergrowth, leading with his head. His preferred method of dispatching enemies, asphyxiation, successful on Officer Kersek, unsuccessful on Sam, strengthens the association. Mitchum's serpentine performance inevitably conjures biblical imagery. As critic J. Hoberman noted, author Barry Gifford used Cape Fear as a location in his novel *Wild at Heart*, and declared Mitchum's Cady, "the angel of death-with-pain, put on earth to give men pause" (Hoberman, 1992, p.10).

De Niro's Cady takes this further by styling himself as an avenging angel, using animal comparisons as a sign of his power. His Cady is not 'just' an animal, telling Lori, "I'm *one hell of* an animal," a remark that doubles as a red flag for the audience. Although snakes are absent from *Cape Fear*, aside from a reference to Cady's granddaddy handling them in church, when seducing Lori he wears a scarlet shirt with a pattern reminiscent of serpent's scales. In a moment of audience dread, Lori mistakes Cady's fury for embarrassment at her mocking of his seemingly limited vocabulary, remarking, "You are now the colour of your shirt." His attire in this scene also evokes images of the Book of Revelation's Great Red Dragon, which associates the character with Francis Dolarhyde, the serial killer from Thomas Harris' *Red Dragon*, another tattooed psychotic with an oral fixation, targeting families for his own sexual satisfaction. Inevitably, Cady's car is a red Mustang convertible, an ostentatious display of his diabolical nature and a boast of his virility. Both are indicated in other scenes: when strip searched, he wears red cheetah briefs, and in the seduction scene with Danielle remarks that he is the big bad wolf, one of the most prominent villains in fairy tales, with the most overtly sexual connotations.

But for Cady, who regards himself as a Nietzschean superman, animal ultimately becomes an insult. As he tells the Bowdens while terrorising them on the houseboat, "Tonight you're gonna learn to be an animal. To live like an animal and to die like one." In his final moments, Cady himself seems to devolve into a more primitive lifeform, lapsing into Pentecostal glossolalia (speaking-in-tongues) when realising death is unavoidable. From his point of view, however, this is a language of the spirit, indicating the character believes he is ascending, even as he is pulled back into the river from whence, the opening credits imply, he came. It is fitting that in his final moments Cady believes down is up; claiming to be Sam's saviour, he tells Danielle that "Every man has to go through Hell to reach his Paradise. You know what Paradise is? Salvation." But his professed saintliness is all surface, much like his taste for Nietzsche. *The Will to Power* and *Thus Spake Zarathustra* look good on the shelf in a prison cell, but his thirst for vengeance does not vibe with Nietzschean philosophy, even if that philosophy today seems as confused as Cady's.

Lesley Stern writes how Jesus' teaching in *The Last Temptation of Christ*, that "God is inside us. The Devil is outside", fits into a discussion of *Cape Fear*, as evidenced in the tattoos that form a large part of Cady's persona (Stern, 1995, p.185-186). It makes sense for the ex-con to be all exterior. A Luciferian figure, he is associated with dazzling light in two early encounters with the Bowdens: first in the cinema and second against a backdrop of fireworks when Leigh spies him sitting on their wall. As created by Scorsese, De Niro and Strick, this Cady could never be the near homunculus of MacDonald's novel. He is a proud Satan, vainglorious in his appearance and autodidactism, both of which he never misses an opportunity to peacock.

Other clues indicate his infernal origins. A penchant for Hawaiian shirts invokes both images of false paradise and a paradise lost. When lasciviously observing a gang of schoolgirls, he wears a red sunset Hawaiian shirt, conversing with Sam in a street lined with palm trees. The shirt reappears when Sam approaches Cady in a restaurant, warning him to leave town, the lawyer having betrayed his oath again by hiring three thugs to attack his nemesis. Hawaiian shirts have denoted a false paradise in previous Scorsese movies. De Niro's Jimmy Doyle sports one when attempting to pick up Liza Minnelli's Francine Evans in *New York, New York*. Their relationship is doomed, partly because Doyle comes across as a proto-Max Cady. As Tom Shone writes, "(De Niro) never made for a convincing Romeo. His Jimmy Doyle hits on Liza Minnelli's Francine in the first scene of *New York, New York* with the relentlessness of a rapist…" (Shone, 2014, p.94). In *The King of Comedy*, Rupert Pupkin wears a Hawaiian shirt for the kidnapping of Jerry Langford for ransom, a madcap scheme to achieve his paradise of appearing on Langford's talk show.

Cady is often associated with the subterranean. First seen performing a final workout before leaving prison, he rises into frame as if from underground. He lures Danielle into the school's basement theatre, and when approaching to kiss her, enters the shot from the bottom of the frame. Of their opening credits, Elaine and Saul Bass said that they and Scorsese wanted to convey, "…a notion of monsters from the deep" (quoted in Wernblad, 2011, p.148). At the end of the film he returns once more to the bottom of the river.

But the most prevalent visual link between *Cape Fear*'s antagonist and the diabolical is fire. Typified by cigars (also enjoyed by Cady in the novel and 1962 movie) and the subsequent plumes of smoke, De Niro's villain is a creature who lives in flame and by extension seems impervious to it. While explaining his mission to "become more than human" to the terrified Leigh and Danielle in the houseboat, he allows molten wax from a lit flare to coat his hand, displaying only the mildest discomfort. Moments after being immolated by Danielle with lighter fluid, he returns to put Sam on trial, visibly scarred but otherwise unimpaired, a twisted baptism in the river returning him reinvigorated.

Fig. 9 Cady demonstrates his tolerance for heat and pain

Alongside appearing first to Leigh against a backdrop of fireworks, Cady later remarks to Sam that his wife is "Hotter than a firecracker on the 4th of July, apparently." When turning Danielle against her father during the theatre seduction scene, he is first spotted lighting a joint with a phallically long flame. He subsequently eats fire when extinguishing the joint on his tongue. It is understandable, then, why Cady would, after finding Sam guilty of placing himself above the law, sentence the lawyer to Dante's ninth circle of Hell. The coldest region of the Inferno because it lies furthest away from God, this is the realm reserved for traitors. At this moment, Cady casts himself as the poet Virgil in Dante's *The Divine Comedy*, making Sam The Pilgrim.

But an indication of how Cady truly sees himself occurs when he tells Sam, "Check out the Bible, Counsellor. Look between Esther and Psalms…". This is The Book of Job, the first appearance of Satan in the Christian Bible, cast as God's servant. In Hebrew, Satan translates as "accuser", a role Cady grants himself. Satan posits to God that the pious Job leads a devout life only because his material comforts permit so. Satan suggests he be allowed to test Job's faith by taking away all the man holds dear. God agrees and Satan takes Job's wealth and slays his children and servants. Blighted by boils and sitting in ashes, Job still refuses to denounce the Lord, even when admonished to do so by his wife.

Here is Cady's promise that Sam will "learn about loss". But, his words to Danielle about Sam's hell leading to salvation belie the corruption motivating his plan. Cady's actions are based solely on destruction; his plan to teach Sam about the loss he experienced when going to prison centres on raping Leigh and Danielle, before presumably murdering the entire family. What salvation there is arrives in a literal *deus ex machina*, as the storm buffets the boat, knocking Cady off his feet and giving the Bowdens the advantage. A higher power also seems to intervene when Sam is about to break the sixth commandment, sweeping Cady back onto the river before Sam can crash a comically large rock down on his tormentor's head. Yet, although redeemed and humbled, Sam is left to ruminate on his experience. His near-stoning of Cady demonstrates how low he has been brought, recalling an earlier scene when he responds to Kersek's suggestion of vigilantism with, "Maybe two thousand years ago we'd have taken this guy out and stoned him to death, but I can't operate outside the law, the law's my business."

"He's denied catharsis," Strick told me, and a line in the earlier draft of his script suggests Sam still has penance to perform: "The blood is still on Sam's hands. It'll be there for a while" (Strick, 1990, p.119). Scorsese allows Sam to wash the blood from his hands: "There is some sort of forgiveness and redemption" (Thompson/Christie, 1996, p.171). But after the ordeal, Sam's life will not match Job's, whose family and servants were returned, plus his wealth in even greater measure. The lawyer's disbarment is a question left hanging, his servants (Graciella and Kersek) remain dead, and there is no guarantee the Bowdens will stay together.

THE FATHER OF LIES

> The demon is a liar. He will lie to confuse us. But he will mix lies with the truth to attack us. The attack is psychological, Damien, and powerful. So don't listen. Remember that – do not listen. – Father Merrin, *The Exorcist* (1973)

Cady as 'the Father of Lies' is best illustrated by his seduction of Danielle in the school theatre. His attack on Lori is simple deception, while with Danielle he acknowledges who he is, but obfuscates his true intentions. Methodically breaking down the girl's barriers, he tempts her with marijuana before flattering her intellectual and sexual curiosity by discussing Henry Miller, then convincing her he did not kill Leigh's dog. Following an assurance that he will not hurt her, Cady subtly encourages the resentment

Danielle feels towards her parents. Asserting he only wishes to help her father, he neglects to mention the violence he has committed. With trust established, Cady violates the girl by inserting his thumb into her mouth and then kissing her. He leaves and she flees the theatre in distressed confusion.

This is a pivotal scene in analysing the success of Scorsese's approach to the material. On one level it is the seduction of a minor by a violent criminal. But this scene, and others in the remake, casts Cady as a Satanic figure, a grand corruptor, shifting the film from dramatic realism into the heightened atmosphere of supernatural horror. Establishing De Niro's villain as an incarnation of mythical evil distances the audience from him, his psychology and, importantly, the pleasure he takes in his actions, although we shall see in Chapter 3 that this reading is not shared by all, with some commentators viewing the seduction scene and the film's politics generally with suspicion.

Fig. 10 Cady mixes the truth with lies to corrupt Danielle

Cady's corruption of Danielle using, as Scorsese puts it, "logic and emotion and psychology very much in the way Satan speaks in the Bible" (Thompson/Christie, 1996, p.166), has a polluting effect on Sam. In her bedroom, disturbed by his daughter's skimpy attire and asking if Cady "touched you", Sam attacks her. Violently covering Danielle's embarrassed smile with his hand, he violates her face, echoing Cady's attack on Lori and implying an incestuous encounter between father and daughter. Cady corrupting Sam also occurs in *The Executioners* and Thompson's original film. In the novel, the lawyer hits dive bars looking for men to kill Cady, then drunkenly embarrasses his wife at a neighbourhood party, ultimately imagining himself performing a lesser version of Cady's crime: "That noble and righteous man. Ah, how he's slipped. Now he goes forth to hire assassins. But, we can't make it easy for him. Because then ole Sam will not be sufficiently aware of his fall from perfect grace. We gotta make him roll in it... Slinking through the slums, picking pockets... They say that any day now he's going to be arrested for indecent exposure" (MacDonald, 1957, p.116). In the 1962 movie, Sam is tempted to gun down Cady after the ex-con terrorises his daughter Nancy (Lori Martin), but is convinced by Peggy that such an action would result in life imprisonment.

Cady's pollution is evident elsewhere in Scorsese's *Cape Fear*. The Bible quote tattoos hint at his messianic complex, while perverting their original meaning. In Matthew 26:18, "My time is at hand" is spoken by Jesus in reference to the crucifixion, but the tattoo implies that the culmination of Cady's revenge is approaching. Romans 12:19's "Vengeance is mine" takes Cady's self-regard further, equating himself with the word of God in the full verse: "Dearly beloved, avenge not yourselves, but *rather* give place unto wrath: for it is written, Vengeance is mine; I will repay, saith the Lord." *Unless* the audience accepts the film's suggestion that Cady is an agent of the Lord, in which case this is a boast about his proximity to the Almighty. By equating himself with God, Cady also debases poetry. A verse by seventeenth-century Catholic priest and mystic Angelus Silesius sounds like a blasphemous appropriation of the Lord's power when Cady bellows:

I am like God and God like me.

I am as large as God, He is as small as I.

He cannot above me, nor I beneath him be.

However, Silesius was referring to the transformative effect of spiritual communion between God and man in the form of contemplative prayer (Chisholm, 1911, p.8). Again, the demon proves himself a liar, using the ambiguities and nuance of religion to cower his enemies.

Speaking at the time of *Mean Streets*, Scorsese said, "I've always been fascinated by the cannibalistic ritual of the Eucharist" (Wilson, 2011, p.38). Cady's cannibalism and oral fixation can be viewed as a diabolical inversion of this ritual, performed as a sin and robbing Danielle and Lori of their innocence. Cannibalism in religion is also linked to betrayal. As Wernblad writes in *The Passion of Martin Scorsese*, *Akhal Kurtza*, the Aramaic word for informer in The Book of Daniel, literally translates as "to eat the flesh of someone else" (2011, p.48). Here Cady turns Sam's perceived 'sin' against Lori, a character close to the lawyer, when he bites a chunk from her cheek.

It is natural that Cady will corrupt food, using it to weaken rather than nourish his enemies. Twice he pays for meals, once for the Bowdens in an ice cream parlour and then for Kersek in a diner when the private eye is tailing him. The ex-con seems to be abiding by Romans 12:20, "Therefore if thine enemy hungers, feed him; if he thirst, give him drink; for in so doing thou shalt heap coals of fire on his head." In Psalm 18:12-14, "coals of fire" refers to divine vengeance. In Romans, the phrase describes the anguish this kindness would cause a person's enemy, forcing them to reflect on their wrongdoing. Understanding Cady's *modus operandi* here is a passive-aggressive conflation of both Psalm and Romans to exert dominance over both Sam and Kersek.

Meta-corruption appears in Gregory Peck's cameo as Cady's lawyer, Lee Heller. In a 180° shift from his Sam Bowden in the original *Cape Fear*, this lawyer displays none of 1962-Bowden's moral sagacity and is wholly deceived by Cady. Heller's white suit recalls the saintly Atticus Finch, providing another layer of despoilment. A more pessimistic interpretation is that this lawyer lives by his surname, *Heller*, and smells his own in the sulfurous Cady. In an example of amusing name play, this Lee is there to chastise Sam for his professional failings, as Leigh does his personal. Completing the inversion is Robert Mitchum's appearance as Lt. Elgart, a lawman who suggests to Sam the vigilante plan Peck formulates in the original movie. Martin Balsam, a police chief in the original film and here elevated to judge, uses the law to weaken this incarnation of Sam Bowden when siding with Cady in a restraining order hearing. Acknowledging the remake's numerous revisions to the story, Peck would tell Wesley Strick, "I just wanted to say that your *Cape Fear* is so much more interesting and exciting and well done than mine" (interview with author).

Fig. 11 New Bowden, old Cady

Fig. 12 And vice versa

ONCE UPON A TIME... "MY REMINISCENCE"

Cady telling Danielle, "Maybe I'm the big bad wolf," most obviously invokes *Little Red Riding Hood*. But there is a biblical connection linking it to the opening narration of *The Night of the Hunter*, and typically for Cady it is none too subtle: "Beware of false prophets, which come to you in sheep's clothing, but inwardly they are ravening wolves" (Matthew 7:15).

Scorsese's film looks back across the centuries for inspiration in its story, modes of narration and the dramatisation of its central monster. The director referred to *Cape*

Fear as a "fairytale [sic] that can be told over and over again, with a moral dilemma which roused my interest…" (Thompson/Christie, 1996, p.165). As Wernblad notes, Danielle's opening words, "My reminiscence," have the feel of "Once upon a time," and there is a fairy-tale style circularity to the film's narration (2011, p.154). Not only do Danielle's words open and close the film, but the opening credits finish with a close-up of her eyes, which shifts from negative red to negative silver to standard photography. The final shot of the film before the end credits, a similar close-up of Danielle's eyes, inverts this, ending on negative red, thus taking us back to the beginning. Choosing to bracket the film with Danielle's narration adds a layer of ambiguity as to who is the story's principal character. We assume Sam, due to screen time and expected practices of Hollywood storytelling. But Danielle's words, especially her final summation, suggest this is equally a tale of her maturation, if not to full womanhood then to a clearer understanding of herself. As she says in the closing moments, "Still, things won't ever be the way they were before he came. But, that's alright, because if you hang onto the past you die a little every day. And for myself, I know I'd rather live. The end…"

Back to *Little Red Riding Hood*. In *The Uses of Enchantment*, his classic psychoanalytical study of fairy tales, Bruno Bettelheim sees the story as staging, "The quandary of standing between the reality principle and the pleasure principle…" (1975, p.171). Using the Brothers Grimm's naming of the character, Bettelheim writes that Little Red Cap's budding sexuality coupled with her immaturity places her in danger. The danger of a naïve sexuality being corrupted is a central theme in *Cape Fear*, expressed in the scene when Cady telephones Danielle, posing as her drama teacher. Although in separate locations, the scene generates unease through the bedroom setting for Danielle, one strap of her nightdress hanging off the shoulder. Cady beguiles her with his apparent 'understanding', saying, "The awkwardness you feel when you're walking down the street and some leering fool's making fun of your sexuality… The anger that you feel, your mom and dad won't let you just grow up and be yourself, be a woman. Go with it. Don't suppress or deny it." Heightening the sense of perniciousness is that Cady delivers this advice while suspended upside down from a door frame, a vampire bat sinking fangs of deceit into the girl.

For Bettelheim, the wolf represents selfish, violent, asocial tendencies that can manifest in the male id. After being lured into the theatre and psychologically manipulated by Cady,

Danielle turns against her parents in their desperate plan to kill him in their home. The death of Graciella (her surrogate mother) is the required shock that reveals to the girl Cady's manipulation of her. A further layer of turmoil is added through Danielle's quasi-Electra Complex, competing with her mother in sexual matters ("You think I've never been flashed before?" she asks Leigh in an early scene). But the film does not suggest Danielle looks to supplant Leigh for herself in Sam's affections, rather that both parents are being rejected for an imagined union with an idealised (and false) father figure, resulting in destructive consequences for which the girl is not prepared.

Little Red Riding Hood's original ending is echoed in *Cape Fear*'s climax. By rushing to her grandmother during a second encounter with the wolf, 'Little Red Cap' is acknowledging she is "by no means mature enough to deal with the wolf (the seducer), and she is ready to settle down to a good working alliance with her mother" (Bettelheim, 1975, p.174). As we shall explore, it is Leigh and Danielle, far more than Sam, who use their resourcefulness to battle Cady on the houseboat. Elsewhere, Bettelheim sees *Little Red Riding Hood*'s father as the superego to the wolf's id. But Sam is unable to adopt this role, having been sentenced to rebuild himself after losing everything. Plus, although mother and daughter are united in their struggle, true to the horror movie this family is not synonymous with security or unity. "We never spoke about what happened. At least not to each other," says Danielle in her closing narration.

It should be noted that this view of female sexuality, as something potentially ruinous unless carefully marshalled, is clearly patriarchal and male chauvinist. That it fits a reading of *Cape Fear* speaks to the film's primary interest in depicting male toxicity, and a relegation of women to illustrate this. Yet, the articulation of this theme also recalls female authorship in one of literature's great examples of man's weakness, vanity and profane ambition, Mary Shelley's *Frankenstein; or, The Modern Prometheus* (1818).

"THE FITTER EMBLEM OF MY CONDITION"

The *Frankenstein* story has had a relatively unacknowledged influence on Martin Scorsese's cinema. After completing *Taxi Driver* the director circled a project called *Haunted Summer*, based on a book by Anne Edwards (Wilson, 2011, p.83). A fictional account of Shelley's writing of *Frankenstein* while holidaying on Lake Geneva with her husband Percy Shelley and friend Lord Byron, a film adaptation was eventually released in 1988, directed by Ivan Passer. Two years earlier, Ken Russell, another director known for Catholic allusions in his work, covered similar material with *Gothic* (1986).

It is unsurprising that key Scorsese films should evoke the spectre of Frankenstein's creation, as Shelley's novel and Scorsese's cinema both convey the spiritual pain of rejection. In *Taxi Driver*, Travis Bickle is spurned by New York City, the place that made him a monster. His attempts to secure a bride are as thwarted as when Frankenstein violently abandons the construction of a mate for the "fiend" in Shelley's novel. Betsy's rejection of Bickle at the porno theatre also carries an echo of Elsa Lanchester's horrified disgust when first seeing Boris Karloff's creature in *The Bride of Frankenstein* (Whale, 1935). Like Shelley's iconic monster, Bickle looks for acceptance but is rejected, and so targets the father figures who wronged him; initially a politician, then the pimp who controls his 'secondary bride', Iris.

Frankenstein reappears in *The King of Comedy*, about which Scorsese said, "The amount of rejection in this film is horrifying" (Ebert, 2008, p.71). Rupert Pupkin regards himself as the creation of late-night talk show host Jerry Langford, turning vengeful when spurned by the unwitting 'father'. This concept even appears in *The Color of Money*. Tom Cruise's Vince experiences the pain of rejection when summarily dumped by Paul Newman's Fast Eddie. Eddie is reunited with his protégé for a pool tournament in Atlantic City, in which Vince takes revenge by being a superior hustler, purposely dumping their match for a bigger payoff. "You used us! You used me!" yells Vince when Eddie later demands his best game. *Cape Fear*'s antagonist also expresses the depth of his pain in being rejected when Sam remains unrepentant for suppressing the evidence.

Sam: You were a *menace*!

Cady: You were my *lawyer*! You *were* my lawyer!

In Shelley's book, the creature compares himself to Milton's Satan, declaring he is "wretched, helpless and alone" (1831 edition, p.132), a remark also describing both Bickle and Pupkin and their place in the world. Rather than Adam, the creature says Satan is "the fitter emblem of my condition" (Shelley, 1831 edition, p.132). The same rings true for Max Cady, who would claim to be The Book of Job's Satan, but is actually "a liar, and the father of lies" to quote Dante's description.

Like Victor Frankenstein, Sam believes he can play God and face no consequences. He places his judgement above the institutions he has sworn to represent, plus the moral and ethical values they embody. Both Frankenstein and Sam abandon their creations, only to see them return years later to wreak havoc when spurned again by the father-nemesis. As with Shelley's tragic hero, Sam's pride results in him underestimating his foe. When admitting to a colleague that he buried the victim report, Sam says of Cady, "...he was an illiterate, I mean I had to read everything to him... There's no way he could know that," not supposing the ex-con may have developed his intellect while incarcerated. Victor's declaration that "There can be no community between you and me; we are enemies" (Shelley, 1831 edition, p.103) finds an analog in Sam's affronted reaction when Cady calls him a colleague: "We're not colleagues. You understand that? We're not colleagues." But Sam and Cady share a kinship in how they have twisted the law to fit their own agenda, as Victor and the creature have a community in their shared knowledge of the other's actions.

Fig. 13 The creature meets his creator

Even Cady's exit from the film, taken back onto the river aboard the raft-like debris of the Bowdens' houseboat, echoes the creature's departure, swept away on an ice-raft, "...and lost in darkness and distance" (Shelley, 1831 edition, p.225). In 1994, De Niro would play the creature in Kenneth Branagh's *Frankenstein*. Although favouring the "wretched, helpless and alone" aspects of the character, De Niro channels Cady's self-righteous rage in the film's final act, murderously teaching Victor about loss, and thereby succeeding where *Cape Fear*'s monster fails.

Beyond Frankenstein, Gothic literature and its feverish offshoot the Southern Gothic are also woven into the fabric of *Cape Fear*. Like the villains of Gothic novels, Cady causes repulsion and fascination in the audience, but crucially not sympathy. As Jonathan Rigby notes, "…in these monsters we see a nightmare reflection of ourselves" (in Bell [ed.], 2013, p.24). MacDonald's description of Cady as "simian" also echoes Robert Louis Stevenson's description of Mr. Hyde attacking someone "…with ape-like fury… trampling his victim under foot, and hailing down a storm of blows" (Stevenson, 1886, p.24), something De Niro's Cady literally does to Sam, his Dr. Jekyll, during the film's climax. However, Rigby's quote does not refer solely to Cady, whose anger we can understand but not condone, and is in fact a better descriptor for Sam. His ethical and moral compromises are more relatable, and after his climactic confrontation with Cady, it is Sam who visually resembles a more devolved form of man, hunched over and long limbed on the riverbank.

The Bowden residence becomes the Old Dark House of Gothic literature and cinema. We never see a secret passageway, but somehow Cady slips in and out of their home undetected, creating a sense of the uncanny that fuels many a Gothic tale. Sam and Leigh's bedroom sits atop their three-storey house, becoming a de facto attic in lieu of seeing the real thing. Marital trauma in an attic summons images of Mrs. Rochester in Charlotte Bronte's *Jane Eyre* (1847), and the subsequent anguish caused by this marital dishonesty.

Crossing the Atlantic, *Cape Fear* is also in the tradition of American Gothic. Annette Wernblad compares it to the work of, among others, Nathaniel Hawthorne (2011, p.146). Hawthorne's *The House of the Seven Gables* (1851) makes a good bedfellow for Scorsese's film, with its themes of guilt, retribution and the cost of sin, the return of a mysterious character after a long prison stretch, a diabolical figure who perverts the law for his own ends, and an implication of the supernatural. While the book's ex-convict is revealed as wrongly accused, Hawthorne's depiction of the true villain of the piece, Judge Pyncheon, demonstrates Cady's lineage to earlier blaggards of Gothic fiction: "The brutish, the animal instincts, as is often the case, had been developed earlier than the intellectual qualities and the force of character, for which he was afterwards remarkable" (Hawthorne, 1851, p.320). The Pyncheon family are locked into a generational feud with the poverty-stricken Maules, who, like Cady (and Freddy Krueger), seem to possess supernatural powers, particularly in dreams: "The Pyncheons... were no better than bond servants to these plebian Maules, on entering the topsy-turvy commonwealth of sleep" (Hawthorne, 1851, p.23). As will recur throughout Gothic fiction and into the yuppie horror films of the 1980s and 1990s, and will be critiqued in *Cape Fear*, the lower class is a terrifying Other for moneyed characters, challenging their way of life and social status.

To Southern Gothic the film also owes an overblown luridness that spirals into a climax of delirium. As Michael Atkinson writes, this is a literary style "contingent on exploiting an entire subculture's historical penchant for vice and self-destruction", teetering on the edge of melodramatic pulp, and fixated on sin, scandal and the inherent rottenness that flourishes in the overripe environs of the South (Atkinson, 2013, p.121). Residual guilt over slavery and bitterness about defeat is encapsulated in Kersek, the gone-to-seed, morally flexible private eye to whom Sam ill-advisedly looks for protection: "You're scared. But that's okay. I want you to savour that fear. The South evolved in fear. Fear of the Indian. Fear of the slave. Fear of the damn union. The South has a fine tradition of savouring fear."

It is worth noting that this is the closest *Cape Fear* comes to addressing the racial tensions that simmer within Southern Gothic. Never a director known for straying too far from the Italian-American or white working-class experience, Scorsese may have felt the confines of a commercial A-picture were not suitable ground on which to tackle the South's history with race. But the film has a noticeably white South, particularly to twenty-first-century audiences. While a handful of African-American extras populate background shots, it is important to note that the remake prominently features the same number of people of colour as the original film (two), and in neither version do they impact the plot. For a Universal Pictures horror movie that dealt with race in 1991, audiences would have needed to turn to Wes Craven's *The People Under the Stairs*, another film that crossed genres (horror, action, social commentary, comedy) and drew on fairy tale conventions.

DEVIL'S ADVOCATES

"THE STORY OF RIGHT HAND, LEFT HAND"

Southern Gothic leads us back to the big screen by way of Robert Mitchum on horseback. De Niro looked to Charles Laughton's *The Night of the Hunter* while researching Cady, who, as we have seen, shares a greater affinity with Mitchum's psychotic preacher Harry Powell than with Mitchum's character in the original *Cape Fear*. Based on Davis Grubb's 1953 novel of the same name, *The Night of the Hunter* incorporates numerous Southern Gothic tropes that would resurface in Scorsese's film. Religious mania, sexual psychosis, and good old-fashioned greed coalesce in Mitchum's Powell, as he chases brother and sister John and Pearl across the heartland of Depression-era America, in pursuit of $10,000 their father stole.

In reimagining Max Cady, *Cape Fear* looks to Mitchum's preacher. A Satanic figure, he too is associated with fire and smoke, and is often illuminated by flame. A clue is in his moniker, 'Old Harry' being one nickname for the Devil. Water is another important element: like the Bowdens, John and Pearl attempt to flee their diabolical foe by taking to the river in a boat, but this only postpones an inevitable showdown. In *Cape Fear*'s opening credits the river is a metaphor for submerged secrets, reflecting Powell's actions when he uses the dark water to hide his most heinous onscreen crime, dumping the body of John and Pearl's mother at the bottom, bound to his Model T-Ford. Grubb's novel has John likening Powell to a bait-stealing gar lurking beneath the surface, described by an old soak John knows as the "Meanest, orneriest, sneakiest son of a bitch in the whole damn river, boy" (1955, p.126). Like Cady and Powell, the gar looks captivating, but is described as being no more than bones and bitterness when John asks if they can eat it.

Powell is another grand corruptor, beguiling townsfolk and twisting religion to accommodate his violent impulses. Like Cady, he "comes not with peace, but with a sword", professing, "the religion the Almighty and me worked out betwixt us". His "sword" takes the form of a switchblade, a phallic substitute that can only bring suffering, as sex manifests in Cady as something solely destructive. As with *Cape Fear*, a dangerous attraction to evil characterises developing female sexuality, most notably in the case of Ruby, a young girl taken in by Lillian Gish's eccentric matron Rachel, who also adopts John and Pearl. Enthralled by the laconic, cold-eyed Powell, even after he is revealed as a murderer Ruby must be course-corrected by Rachel, who is wiser to the exploitable desires of young women. Mother and daughter figures forming an alliance link this back to *Little Red Riding Hood*'s ending, and flows into *Cape Fear*'s characterisation of female sexuality.

The Night of the Hunter too shrouds its villain with an aura of the supernatural. "Don't he ever sleep?" complains John as their tormentor relentlessly pursues them. Taking this notion of malevolent ability further, Lesley Stern wonders if the shimmering silhouette in Elaine and Saul Bass' credits for *Cape Fear* resembles Mitchum's Cady (1995, p.208). But, more than the 1962-Cady, this seems to be Harry Powell's shadow cast across Scorsese's movie. The silhouette's left hand is prominently extended, recalling the "HATE" tattoo Powell has inked on the fingers of his left hand, with "LOVE" on the right. As with Cady, body art here is rooted in fundamentalist religion, Powell using the tattoos to captivate strangers with his tale of Cain and Abel and "the story of right hand, left hand". Cain slew his brother with the left hand, and when judging the saved from the sinful, Jesus grouped those bound for "everlasting fire" on his left-hand side (Matthew 25:41). When it comes to retribution, Cady would obviously think himself a southpaw.

Fig. 14 Harry Powell professes love, but brings hate in The Night of the Hunter © *Paul Gregory Productions/MGM*

Harry Powell is one of Classical Hollywood's great villains, realised by Mitchum under the direction of Charles Laughton. For over 30 years Laughton was married to Elsa Lanchester, who portrayed both Mary Shelley and the creature's appalled mate in James Whale's *The Bride of Frankenstein*. Like the original *Frankenstein*, Whale's sequel was made by Universal, the studio which released the famous monster movies of the Classical period, plus the two versions of *Cape Fear*. Apposite that Max Cady should share the same studio as this rogue's gallery; in many ways he is an amalgam of these earlier characters. Besides Frankenstein's creature he possesses the lycanthropic qualities of the Wolf Man, and the Invisible Man's megalomania and ability to move undetected. Like the Mummy he has lain unseen for a protracted length of time, and emerges from the swamp like the Creature from the Black Lagoon. With the Phantom he shares a penchant for the operatically overblown, and is imbued with the malevolent charm of Lugosi's Dracula, although a better comparison is Christopher Lee's Count; Scorsese's comments on Lee's interpretation matching his approach to Cady: "Having been reared on Bela Lugosi, with whom you knew you were in trouble, Lee seemed like a very sensible, sophisticated gentlemen. So that later on, when… Dracula turns up, eyes bloodshot, in an extreme close-up, it was absolutely terrifying" (Thompson/Christie, 1996, p.103).

To close the chapter we will shift forward to the 1980s and two sub-genres useful for analysing this cine-literate film: the slasher film and the yuppie-in-peril cycle. Wesley Strick said the slasher movie was not on his mind when writing the script, but *Cape Fear* demonstrates how ingrained slasher conventions were in American horror cinema of the early 1990s. Scorsese's film was released in November 1991; in September, the Elm Street saga had apparently closed with *Freddy's Dead* (Talalay, 1991). Inevitably, Robert Englund's Freddy Krueger would be resurrected for *Wes Craven's New Nightmare* (Craven, 1994) and *Freddy vs. Jason* (Yu, 2003).

Like Krueger, Cady is a sexual predator back for revenge after a civilised society punishes him with vigilante justice. He haunts the Bowdens even in their slumber: when half-asleep in his bed Sam suddenly sees his nemesis in the room, and Danielle awakens from a nightmare during the segment when Cady is being baited to invade the family home. In the closing narration she says she "hardly dreams about him anymore…". As with Michael Myers and Jason Voorhees of the *Halloween* and *Friday the 13th* franchises,

Cady dances with the uncanny. Both slasher icons survive fatal wounds and while the *Friday the 13th* series ultimately confirms Jason Voorhees as a supernatural entity, *Halloween* keeps it ambiguous.

The slasher cycle took a machete to the supposed sanctity of American suburbia, typically setting its story around a calendar holiday or seasonal event. J. Lee Thompson would himself helm *Happy Birthday to Me* (1981), whose poster featured a tag line boasting, "Six of the most bizarre murders you will ever see." Scorsese's *Cape Fear* is set around the 4th of July, the holiday offering ironic commentary to the story. Is this Independence Day Cady's liberation from prison, or his belief that he is saving Sam from past transgressions? Or, through the shock therapy of their ordeal, the Bowdens' liberation from the grievances that plague them? Whatever the motivation, as with slasher villains Cady ultimately ruins the calendar holiday. In *The Making of Cape Fear*, Strick says, "The idea of Cady turning up at this 4th of July parade was a way of poisoning the very heart of America" (Bouzereau, 2001).

Cape Fear's climactic showdown largely adheres to the slasher film's Final Girl narrative device. Sam is bound and emasculated, and a scripted moment when he goes overboard and heroically climbs back onto the houseboat was cut (Strick, 1990, p.109). Leigh and Danielle must use their intelligence and resourcefulness to battle Cady alone, although this is not a one-for-one translation with the Final Girl climax. With no room on the houseboat for exciting suspense set-pieces, we dread that Cady is going to enact his revenge, forcing us to witness his rape of the mother and daughter. The film spares us this, and in Danielle's immolation of Cady borrows one of Nancy's moves in battling Freddy Krueger during the climax of *A Nightmare on Elm Street*. A focus on character over suspense mechanics highlights a defining tension: visually the climax resembles the lurid pyrotechnics of a slasher movie, yet Leigh's diversionary tactic is to plead with Cady that he rape only her and spare Danielle. A moment electrified by Jessica Lange's performance, it nevertheless shifts the film away from the emotionally easier, more physical denouement of glossy Hollywood thrillers, or even slasher titles such as *A Nightmare on Elm Street*, *Halloween*, and *The Slumber Party Massacre* (Jones, 1982).

Cady dies at the end of 1991's *Cape Fear*. Yet, from his calm expression as the wreckage pulls him beneath the river's surface, the audience feels he is merely biding time like a Michael or a Jason. Danielle's closing narration implies his presence lingered within the family long after his demise. If not quite the slasher convention Robin Wood identified when writing that if the monster is defeated then the heroine is left insane, it nevertheless suggests Cady's malevolence has survived. This disquieting exit was at the suggestion of Robert De Niro. Strick had scripted an epilogue based on a scene from *The Executioners*, in which Sam sees Cady's lifeless body and realises he has "turned this elemental and merciless force into clay, into dissolution" (MacDonald, 1957, p.192). Strick recounted to me, "In my epilogue scene Cady's body is just dredged up on a hook with some sort of device that pulls him out of the water, and he's just waterlogged and upside down and very dead." He went onto explain, "[De Niro] asked that it be removed… he felt that the audience didn't want to see Cady reduced to that, even in death… Of course, the essence of the horror villain is this implacable creature that is unstoppable. So it would be like pulling the rug from under all the power that you've taken great pains to dramatise through the two hours of the movie" (interview with author).

DESIGNER FABLES

The yuppie horror sub-genre began with Scorsese's *After Hours* in 1985. Although yuppies-in-peril movies would appear after *Cape Fear* (e.g. *Single White Female* [Schroeder, 1992], *The Temp* [Holland, 1993]), Scorsese's remake resembles a *fin-de-siècle*.

The social parents of today's 'early adopters', the middle-class-and-rising yuppies of the 1980s defined themselves through materialism and status. Usefully, characters in yuppie horror live aspirational lifestyles that audiences can admire, while also savouring the spectacle of that lifestyle being ripped apart. These characters are typically liberal, but must reevaluate assumptions when confronted by a force that threatens their all-important standing. Reflecting the 1980s boom-and-bust economy (and the concerns of Gothic literature), threats in the yuppie horror film include being usurped by/joining an underclass and bankruptcy and/or property divestiture. Cady's promise that "You're gonna learn about loss" is the mission statement for psychos in yuppie horror movies. In films such as *Something Wild* (Demme, 1986), *Fatal Attraction* (Lyne, 1987), *Bad Influence*

(Hanson, 1990), *Pacific Heights* (Schlesinger, 1990) and *The Hand That Rocks the Cradle* (Hanson, 1992), the true horror comes in realising, "once you leave the bourgeois life, you're immediately prey to crime, madness, squalor, poverty" (Powers, quoted in Grant, 1998, p.282). But, the protagonist usually ends the film like Job, with their home, possessions and relationships returned, more or less. Characters are as successful, or more successful, than when the film began, having experienced temporary grave material and/or professional difficulties to ensure a lesson is learnt.

Cape Fear goes beyond most films in this cycle by making good on the antagonist's mission statement. To paraphrase Scorsese, when watching *Fatal Attraction* or *Bad Influence*, you root for villains Glenn Close and Rob Lowe to strip 'heroes' Michael Douglas and James Spader of all they have, then dump their self-absorbed, cowardly backsides on the street. Those films are incoherent texts, insisting their leads are flawed but likeable, no matter how shabby their depicted behaviour. Scorsese is unafraid to populate his films with unsympathetic characters, and, through twenty-four rewrites, deemed this essential to *Cape Fear*'s success. His primary concern is with the spiritual aspects of the Bowdens' journey. He is unconcerned that their houseboat is destroyed, or that they are unlikely to remain in a residence that hosted two murders. He is similarly indifferent to whether Sam loses his job after having Cady assaulted, one of the worst things that could happen in a yuppie horror film. What matters is that through their trials the characters experience an epiphany. Even more important than reaching Paradise is that sins of the past are confronted and acknowledged. Interestingly, economic anxiety *was* a feature in MacDonald's *The Executioners*, with Sam's worries about mortgage payments and a lack of savings exacerbated by the financial strain of hiring a private eye to tail Cady.

The yuppie horror film's antagonist is a shadowy reflection of the protagonist, a narrative device with which we have seen Scorsese is familiar. In the director's work, this shadow can be located within the same character or a second male character, "...a kind of twisted Jiminy Cricket who will not let (the protagonist) complacently lie to himself" (Wernblad, 2011, p.11).

Rob Lowe in *Bad Influence* and Jennifer Jason Leigh in *Single White Female* are the id, casting a light on James Spader and Bridget Fonda's self-delusion. Same too for Ray

Liotta, Henry Hill himself, to Jeff Daniels in *Something Wild*. Glenn Close in *Fatal Attraction* is a walking reminder of the weakness and guilt Michael Douglas has within him. She also lives in the meat-packing district, personifying the social fall Douglas' character faces if his adultery is exposed. Cady neatly fits this shadowy Other, right down to many antagonists in yuppie horror films dwelling below ground. Rebecca De Mornay's vengeful nanny in *The Hand That Rocks the Cradle* has an M.O. similar to Cady's, and lives in the basement room of a spacious residence housing the family she plans to steal from Annabella Sciorra. De Mornay is defeated when Sciorra hurls her out of the attic window, literally casting her down. Spader shoots Lowe off a pier at the end of *Bad Influence*, sending him to the murky depths of the controlled repressed. These shadow characters also share Cady's apparent supernatural ability, unfettered by laws of physics, particularly Lowe, who seemingly bends time with the rapidity at which he can dismantle elements of Spader's life.

Sam first interacts with Bowden in a movie theatre, a place that literally projects light and shadow. In that 'August 31, 1990' draft, the film playing is a yuppie comedy in which "two young stockbrokers, man and woman, trade double-entendres" (Strick, 1990, p.4). *Cape Fear* swaps this for *Problem Child*, and a scene that riffs on the "Here's Johnny!" moment from *The Shining*. This Tinseltown reflection of the Bowdens' dysfunction is rudely interrupted by Max Cady, here to remind Sam that his problems cannot be as easily resolved. Later, the ex-con informs the lawyer he too had a wife and daughter, both now lost to him. He also takes the opportunity to indulge in a little more of the uncanny when suggesting he has returned from the grave: "My daughter, don't even know me. Her momma told her I was dead, which in a way I was..." When Cady is strip searched in the police station, Scorsese moves the camera from one side of the one-way mirror to the other in a way that confuses what is real and what is reflection.

Cady repeatedly reminds Bowden he too is well-versed in the law ("Here we are: two lawyers for all practical purposes talking shop") and is not shy in revealing his intentions to usurp Sam ("If you're not better than me then I can have what you have… a wife, a daughter"). Through his self-improvement, Pentecostal cracker Cady represents that underclass threatening to appropriate Sam's upper-middle-class status. But he is the shadow, so plans to fulfil his ambitions will be the darkest imaginable, taking what he covets only to ruin it. When fighting Sam on the swampy riverbank after destroying the houseboat and terrorising the Bowdens, Cady cannot resist one more comparison: "Well here we are, Counsellor, just two lawyers working it out!" On the riverbank, Cady also remarks, "You've already sacrificed me, Counsellor," possibly suggesting that Sam has passed his trial, and that the intervention that spares the Bowdens was from a satisfied higher power. But, as mentioned, while there may have been salvation, paradise is lost, and who knows for how long.

Here we have examined the ways in which *Cape Fear* relies on conventions of horror cinema and literature, and how they unite with the director's own themes and preoccupations. The fantastical portrayal of its sexually sadistic antagonist has a distancing effect that allows Cady to operate within a big budget studio movie. But *Cape Fear* generated fierce criticism upon release. The film remains controversial, with elements of its production now no longer permissible. In the following chapter we examine those criticisms, the film's sexual politics, and its treatment of sexual violence.

Chapter 3: Troubled Waters – Sexual Politics in *Cape Fear*

Female representation in Martin Scorsese's films has remained a point of contention throughout his career, up to and including his most recent release as of writing, 2019's *The Irishman*. In that film, the damning silence of Anna Paquin's character, playing the onscreen daughter to Robert De Niro's mobster, was regarded by some as another example of Scorsese denying female characters a voice.

Yet the furore that marked *Cape Fear*'s US release was second only to that during production and release of *The Last Temptation of Christ*. Criticisms of *Cape Fear*'s depiction of women, sexual violence and sexual threat continue into the twenty-first century. "It's everything that is wrong with the world," is how a thirtysomething female friend described the film to me. Which seems an appropriate point to acknowledge that I write this as a white, middle-class, middle-aged male. From necessity rather than choice, this chapter (and the entire book) is refracted through that lens. While I attempt to avoid an unconscious bias, inevitably this commentary will be gendered.

But the aim of this chapter is to analyse the different factors that inform the film's depiction of women and sexual threat, and to review those accusations of misogyny. It is not the author's intention to champion it as a work of progressive feminism – notwithstanding his ongoing examination of destructive masculinity, Scorsese is a director who privileges a male point of view, which inevitably affects the level of agency granted to female characters.

Released in November 1991, *Cape Fear* arrived amidst a socio-political uproar over sexual violence in the US. Judge Clarence Thomas was elected by a narrow margin to the Supreme Court on 15th October, following allegations of sexual harassment from Anita Hill when Thomas was her supervisor. At the time of the film's release, the high-profile rape trial of William Kennedy Smith, nephew to John F. Kennedy, was weeks away. Smith would controversially be acquitted of all charges on 11th December. Also raging in the social discussion was the topic of date rape, alongside the emergence of 'political correctness' as a cultural movement. The early 1990s also saw a continuation of the backlash against the second-wave feminism that rose in the 1970s and continued into the 1980s. In *The New Avengers: Feminism, femininity and the rape-revenge cycle*, Jacinda Read argues *Fatal Attraction* was "…perhaps the seminal backlash text of the period" for the way it demonises the successful, independent, sexually active businesswoman who grew in cultural prominence during the decade (2000, p.206). Scorsese's film was perhaps destined to create controversy, but it entered a perfect storm of cultural and political argument.

According to the feature "Who's Afraid of *Cape Fear*?" in the February 1992 issue of *Empire*, the film became "…the hot political potato in the US…" and "…some critics are now citing *Cape Fear* as Scorsese's own personal backlash against the entire feminist/PC movement in the US" (1992, p.6). Conversely, critic Pam Cook remarked: "A deafening silence surrounds the sexual politics of Scorsese's *Cape Fear*… a violent rape movie in which women apparently collude in their own punishment at the hands of a rapist," arguing, "…critics, even when shocked by the film's brutality, prefer to discuss it in formal and/or moral terms – as 'cinema' or as a treatise on good and evil" (1992, p.14). Echoing this is David Greven in *Psycho-Sexual: Male Desire in Hitchcock, De Palma, Scorsese, and Friedkin*: "The critical indifference to the misogyny of works like *Cape Fear*, in which, with entirely gratuitous violence, the villain bites off the cheek of the protagonist's mistress… reveals the entrenched biases of film criticism" (2013, p.267).

Less criticised upon release was the sexual threat directed at the 15-year-old Danielle. On a related point, the advent of the #MeToo movement in 2017 highlighted Hollywood's widespread neglect of issues around consent, foreknowledge and the safeguarding of actors (particularly female actors). While no-one has ever reported being harmed on *Cape Fear*, we shall discuss one aspect of its production that timestamps it as a film made long before this change in industry standards.

Reviewing the sexual politics of *Cape Fear* requires an analysis of Scorsese's approach to dramatising male toxicity, the influence of his Catholicism, his methods of depicting violence, the tropes of contemporary US horror, and his and De Niro's commitment to authenticity. In a 1976 interview with Roger Ebert, Scorsese speaks of the "goddess-whore complex", saying, "You're raised to worship women, but you don't know how to approach them on a human level, on a sexual level" (Ebert, 2008, p.44).

Male discomfort with women and female sexuality has been a constant within Scorsese's work. 1967's *Who's That Knocking at My Door* plays like a compendium of Catholic-induced sexual hang-ups, with Harvey Keitel's J.R. steeped in a religious guilt that manifests whenever he attempts intimacy with his new girlfriend. That the film credits his girlfriend, played by Zina Bethune, as 'The Girl' also indicates the filmmaker would rather place her on a pedestal than develop her character. A layer of complexity is added to the narrative when J.R. rejects 'The Girl' after she confides in him that she is a rape survivor. When realising he cannot ignore his feelings, he tells her, "I forgive you." Refusing his ignorant attempt at compassion, 'The Girl' tells J.R. to leave, at which he calls her a "whore", before attempting another reconciliation that is once again rebuffed. J.R.'s subsequent church confession is intercut with statues of saints' brutal martyrdom, forming a connection between sexual desire and punishment that echoes throughout Scorsese's filmography.

This same impotence and guilt when confronted with the Madonna-whore figure (or figures) occurs in *Taxi Driver* and *Raging Bull*. Both films feature a lead male who worships a 'pure goddess' character, before sullying her – Travis Bickle by taking Betsy to a porno theatre then angrily confronting her when she refuses to see him again, Jake La Motta through seeing infidelity in every interaction his wife Vickie has with another man, ultimately beating her for an imagined betrayal. Bickle subsequently attempts to restore purity to Iris, a child the city has turned into a whore, by slaying the pimp and gangsters who profit from her. Undercutting his apparent heroics is the critical distance Scorsese employs in depicting the obvious psychosis of a man society will then champion as a hero. These female characters highlight destructive male impulses. But their motivations and responses to situations do not classify them as Madonna or whore, and they are shown to be undeserving of the treatment they receive. Which remains scant comfort to viewers wanting a more developed female character, or a depiction of how religion comforts/torments the other 51% of the population.

Conflicted opinions about sex, women and Judeo-Christian religion go directly to source in *The Last Temptation of Christ*, which features both Mary, Mother of Jesus and Mary Magdalene. In an echo of the porno theatre scene from *Taxi Driver*, Jesus visits Magdalene's house and sits with her customers, all of whom watch her having intercourse while they wait (a moment not in Kazantzakis' novel). Scorsese commented,

"The scene isn't done for titillation; it's to show the pain on her face, the compassion Jesus has for her as he fights his sexual desire for her" (quoted in O'Brien, 2018, p.138). Once again, the conflation of sexual desire with spiritual torment and punishment, once more originating within the conflicted male psyche. Scorsese adds a further layer to the intertwining of sex and sin by having Barbara Hershey, the actor who portrays Magdalene, voice a serpent that tempts Jesus. His rejection of it marks the beginning of an understanding of his divinity. Not that Hershey was a mere actor-for-hire on the film; she introduced the director to the book when they were shooting *Boxcar Bertha* (Wilson, 2011, p.146).

Key to the filmmaker's exploration of masculinity in crisis is an examination of this fear of intimacy, a theme typically depicted through a character's paranoid inability to navigate a world closing in on them (e.g. *Mean Streets*, *Taxi Driver*, *Raging Bull*, *After Hours*), or a fall from grace due to excessive pride and/or greed (e.g. *New York, New York*, *Goodfellas*, *New York Stories* and later *Casino* (1995) and *The Departed*). In both cases the male characters are seeking salvation, but their journey is marked by distrust, betrayal and violence, usually directed at those closest to them, characters who are often women.

Cape Fear fits this latter category. Within the film's moral and ethical framework, Sam Bowden is a personification of Mark 8:36, "For what shall it profit a man, if he shall gain the whole world, and lose his own soul?" On the surface, Sam seems more sexually mature than the typical Scorsese male to this point in the director's career, and less physically violent. But he shares the same flaws. Through his adultery he broke a spiritual vow just as he broke an ethical vow in omitting evidence in Cady's trial. He begrudges Leigh's bitterness at his infidelity, while being attracted to younger, more pliable women, embodied in the legal clerk, Lori. He denies Lori her adulthood by telling her they should cool their relationship in language more befitting a father having a sex-ed talk with a child: "When two people get married and they live together for a *long* time…"

Sam can only assert physical dominance over younger women, Lori on the squash court and when wrestling with Danielle in an ice cream parlour. He reveals an instinctive male chauvinism when appointing himself Leigh's intellectual and moral guardian, choosing not to tell her Cady was incarcerated for rape ("I thought you said it was battery?"). Danielle's developing intellect and sexuality is resented because it lays beyond his control. Unlike in the book and 1962 film, Sam (and Leigh) do not discuss Cady's crimes with their daughter. This lack of trust emanates from Sam, making the unified Bowdens of the earlier versions an impossibility here. He is uncomfortable with Danielle's developing body and reacts violently to a suspected sexual encounter with Cady, when a frank discussion of the ex-con's crimes would have been more effective. The pragmatism of the less progressive sixties has been abandoned with nothing to replace it.

We have seen Scorsese was instrumental in bringing this dysfunction to the script, doubling down on the bitterness and resentment. As he told Richard Schickel, "It really did start for me as pure entertainment, but then I changed it to be about the dissolution of the family unit" (2011, p.193-4). The director was at the end of his fourth marriage while making *Cape Fear*, divorcing the film's producer Barbara De Fina and establishing a relationship with Illeana Douglas, although his professional relationship with De Fina did continue, most recently collaborating on 2016's *Silence*. It is not difficult to imagine, then, that real-life events influenced the film's guilt and pessimism over male/female relationships. Some viewers have read the end of the film as the family reunited, but Scorsese is wary of their future: "Yes, they're back together, but think about what they're going to be like afterwards" (Schickel, 2011, p.197).

Overlap also exists with Scorsese's more overtly personal films in the way Sam implicitly regards women as property. Jake La Motta dictates Vickie's every movement. In *Goodfellas*, Tommy DeVito tells his girlfriend (played by Illeana Douglas) in kidding-*not*-kidding fashion, "I'm gonna go see Stacks... Look straight ahead or I'll fucking kill ya." Sam's belief in his ownership of Leigh and Danielle is suggested through the dialogue of his shadow, Max Cady: "If you're not better than me then I can have what you have... a wife, a daughter." Freudian readings of the film extend this to Sam transferring an incestuous desire for Danielle onto Cady. *Cape Fear* certainly exists in a post-Freudian world, where the filmmakers and characters alike will be familiar with the psychoanalytical concepts. But labelling the film another telling of the Freudian family romance removes the richer explorations of ethical and moral compromise, and concepts of punishment and redemption. Plus, this point of view subjects the women to a male gaze that we shall see the film largely avoids.

Rather than a parable about incestuous desires within a family, the film seems to present a pessimistic treatise on male/female relationships. The viewpoint is patriarchal, but implicit is a caustic critique of a male-dominated world, one where sex is weaponised and intimacy is expressed at a character's peril. Within this, Leigh, Danielle and Lori resist the property label applied to them, and the Madonna-whore categorisation of women in other Scorsese films. With regards to Leigh, a significant part of this is due to Jessica Lange's work with Wesley Strick. As previously mentioned, Strick told me Lange was candid about her dissatisfaction with the role as written, and Scorsese assured her she would have the writer's services to "…help her find the character that is more layered". Lange's casting was a shrewd move. An accomplished actor, she quickly grew beyond the 'imperilled Pauline' of her debut movie, *King Kong* (Guillermin, 1976). She won her first Oscar playing it light in *Tootsie* (Pollack, 1982), but during the 1980s would distinguish herself through impressive depictions of femininity-in-crisis, with such films as *The Postman Always Rings Twice* (Rafelson, 1981), *Frances* (Clifford, 1982), *Crimes of the Heart* (Beresford, 1986) and *Music Box* (Costa-Gavras, 1989).

Alongside her work with Strick, Lange's presence and reputation does much of the film's heavy lifting in its depiction of women. Leigh is not idealised by Sam, nor is she an ephemeral object to be discarded. Leigh is a survivor of betrayal, someone rebuilding her life with a man who continually acts in untrustworthy ways. In my discussion with the screenwriter, he mentioned something that indicated the politics of the time: "(Leigh) was seething with rage at (Sam's) behaviour and she was punishing him, and we had to find ways for her to do that without alienating the audience." The consensus in 1991 was that mothers in movies ultimately must be sympathetic. Leigh's pain could be shown, but even within a family this damaged she could only castigate her husband so far.

The character also displays traits associated with the independent woman that conservatives were attempting to suppress. Leigh is educated, intelligent, has a white collar, economically rewarding job (graphic design), albeit one where she works from home, and she is not solely motivated by housekeeping and child-rearing. As Read notes, the early 1990s saw a conservative call for "more traditional models of gender (otherwise known as the backlash)" in the US and UK, the UK describing it as a return to "Victorian values" (2000, p.187). Hollywood's caution around presenting female empowerment while not upsetting the economic apple cart was evident in *Thelma and Louise* (Scott, 1991) writer Callie Khouri having to reassure audiences, "The issues surrounding the film are feminist. But the film itself is not" (quoted in Read, 2000, p.103).

Cape Fear does not suggest the family's problems lay in Leigh's career or the anger she feels for Sam. In fact it suggests the opposite, that she would be happier without her husband. Yet there is a tension in the depiction of Leigh. She never leaves the house unless with her family or performing a parental duty (driving Danielle to school). Read writes how rape-revenge films back to the silent era would define the home as a feminine space and outside the home as masculine. Sam operates within multiple external 'masculine' spaces: his office, a police station, the squash court. Leigh almost entirely resides within the feminine space of the home (including the houseboat). A scene in which she visits Sam's office to discuss their marital crisis was shot but cut from the finished film.

As a counterargument, if reading *Cape Fear* as a horror film it makes sense to keep the family chiefly associated with the home. This is the sanctuary that Sam has diseased, infecting it via his professional failings and subsequent moral weakness. An uneasy line of reasoning perhaps (horror is replete with examples running against it), but *Cape Fear* does favour the home (and its proxy the houseboat) above all other locations. But job or not, Leigh being chiefly housebound, coupled with Cady's revenge mission targeting her and Danielle for rape, places the film's politics within an earlier age of gender roles. Given the source novel and the original film being products of the 1950s and 1960s, to a degree this is unsurprising. Yet there is director influence here also. Scorsese *is* more interested in *Cape Fear*'s male protagonist and antagonist. At the time of UK release, *Empire*'s feature on the film included the following:

> 'The films I'm dealing with have often been about men's worlds, where the women seem to be adjuncts,' admits Scorsese, flashing a quick glance of displeasure. 'I think the women in *Goodfellas* and *Raging Bull* are very strong, but they're not in the *ring*. In general, I have to be true to the society in which the film operates. I don't think it's right to overbalance it just for the sake of trying to be politically correct.' (Gleiberman, 1992, p.64)

And in a Scorsese movie, the society in which the film operates will invariably be male.

Alice Doesn't Live Here Anymore, the director's first studio assignment, may be his only female-led movie, but the expressionistic style of 1940s and 1950s 'women's pictures' permeates his work. Before this bestows accidental feminist credentials upon him, remember that those pictures were chiefly directed by men. Scorsese directly quotes Douglas Sirk in *Cape Fear* when *All That Heaven Allows* (1955) plays silently on the TV while the Bowdens, Kersek and Graciella await the arrival of Max Cady. Beyond a title hinting at the Old Testament machinery powering Cady's vendetta, *All That Heaven Allows*' story of a middle-aged woman (Jane Wyman) causing scandal by courting a younger man (Rock Hudson) is an indictment of the hypocrisy within WASP communities and families, something close to the heart of Scorsese's remake, with *Cape Fear* resembling a dark inversion of Sirk's film. Rock Hudson is the good angel to Cady's Satan, creating mini-Edens in his job as a tree surgeon, and whose credo, "To thine own self be true", finds darker meaning in the ex-con.

Of rape-revenge narratives in melodrama, Read writes, "…for female characters rape is represented as both a result of, and a violation of, their femininity and for male characters as a violation of their masculine ability to protect women" (2000, p.94). This categorisation finds common ground with Cady's desire to have what Sam has and Sam's inability to protect his family (or property). Yet rape-revenge narratives of the classical period carried a tacit reminder of a woman's societal role as wife and mother. These and later conservative films in the cycle would present rape as punishment for the woman straying beyond assigned feminine duties. In *Cape Fear* Leigh and Danielle are collateral damage of Sam's transgressions, which reduces their agency but the film does not punish them for ambitions beyond traditional feminine roles. Whether highlighting crises in masculinity is any improvement on the politics of those earlier films is something for the individual viewer to decide.

The saturated colours and elevated emotional register of *Cape Fear* owes much to 1950s melodrama, which often teetered on the verge of Gothic. Negative reaction to the film may also emanate from the presentation of inflammatory themes and events in this style. Another point of controversy is whether the women in the film collude with Cady, thereby orchestrating a sexual threat against themselves. Pam Cook notes that in terms of numbers, men come off worse than women in the film, but rightly concludes women are the film's obvious victims. Reasons for this include an omnipresent sexual dread (the depiction of Sam and Leigh's coitus that literally turns negative, Sam's discomfort at his daughter's developing sexuality) combined with an atmosphere of sexual menace.

In the April 1992 *Sight and Sound* article, 'Scorsese's Masquerade', Cook took both the film and director to task. She saw a troubling complicity in the film's women, writing, "*Cape Fear*'s complex pattern of refracted images makes it plain that avenging angel Cady is acting on behalf of victimised women. In this light, the female characters' apparent collusion in their own humiliation – the fact that they are attracted to the rapist – takes on a different hue" (1992, p.15). Cook's analysis diverges from mine on this point. To quote Kersek in the film, "Cady's an opportunist." Any connection he attempts to form with the Bowden women is depicted as the connivance of a malevolent and corrupting influence attacking the family at its weakest spot, their lack of trust in one another.

We have already seen how Cady preys upon Danielle's naivete and how Leigh's post-coital frustration could be read as summoning the ex-con. On this latter point, Jessica Lange said she played Leigh in the scene as a woman who is, "at a point where everything's feeling empty. There's this kind of sensual, even more than sexual, sensual yearning to be connected to something. So, I don't think, and I didn't play it, that it was directed toward Cady" (Bouzereau, 2001). Of the same scene, Scorsese commented, "It's as if the husband doesn't exist and she's going out on a date – but unfortunately the date is with Max" (Maslin, 1991, p.15). So a sexual link exists in the director's mind between Leigh and Cady, but the scene itself suggests a frustration in Lange's character, rather than desire for a masochistic encounter with a rapist.

Also important is Leigh's interaction with Cady when he returns the dog collar. Testament to Lange's input into the movie, the scene was included late in pre-production after she noticed Leigh, like Peggy in the 1962 original, had no dialogue scene with Cady until the finale (they are both in the cinema, but do not meet). This scene does not appear in the 'August 31, 1990' draft, which moves from a gardening scene with Danielle and Graciella, which was shot but cut, to Kersek telling Sam that Cady made him for a private investigator. In this late addition, Leigh displays the bitter knowledge she routinely demonstrates when dealing with the duplicity or vanity of the male characters. Recognising Cady for what he is, she tells him, "Oh, there is gonna be more, isn't there, Mr. Cady? You won't stop until you're happy… I wanted to know what you looked like; I've been waiting to see your face. But, you know, now that I see you, you are just repulsive."

Rather than a story of collusion, *Cape Fear* can be read as a warning to the female characters about the dangers of sexual awakening within a patriarchy. With cropped hair and a wardrobe comprising almost exclusively of slacks and loose, shapeless blouses, Leigh rejects a more sexualised femininity. We can presume this is due to her disappointment and disgust with Sam's actions. Her late-night application of lipstick seems more an attempt to bring colour into her own life rather than to beautify herself for a man. Traditional femininity here is synonymous with sexual callowness; both the more femininely presented Danielle and Lori lose their innocence after being exposed to male deception and violence.

Having to sacrifice aspects of their femininity seems predestined in their ambiguously gendered names – Leigh, Danielle, Lori – a trait shared with many a Final Girl in slasher movies. Staying with the slasher film, *Cape Fear*'s climax lifts tropes from both that sub-genre and the rape-revenge narrative. Sam is symbolically emasculated, bound for much of Cady's assault, making Leigh and Danielle's experience facing the monster analogous to that of the Final Girl. The gender fluidity of slasher movies, particularly the masculinisation of the Final Girl as she confronts the monster, appears here by way of the lighter fluid Danielle stuffs down the front of her jeans, then produces to immolate Cady when he lights an equally phallic cigar. This is also Danielle's response to the handgun Cady has earlier tucked down the front of his jeans. During the climax, the women use delaying or diversionary tactics until they can grasp the opportunity to escape Cady, with Sam only showing force in a final fight with his nemesis, after the women have saved themselves.

Physical contact of any kind in the film rarely comforts. Cady employs it only to assert power through assault and rape. In violating Danielle, he corrupts intimacy when caressing her face, slipping his thumb into her mouth, and kissing her. As mentioned, Sam uses physical contact to establish dominance over Danielle and Lori. Lovemaking for Leigh is shown to be devoid of warmth, and Leigh's physical contact with Sam is almost

Fig. 15 Danielle's phallic retort to Cady's menace

solely reserved for when she strikes him in anger. In a comic aside, this has become such a default setting for their relationship that she instinctively slaps him when Sam awakens her to say he thinks Cady is already inside the house. The only physical embrace of genuine warmth is when Leigh hugs Danielle after Cady has been vanquished. A suggestion here perhaps that traditional gender roles are being endorsed, with Leigh's character arc being a recognition of her maternal responsibilities. Mother and daughter's fractious relationship only begins to heal after Cady has revealed his true nature by killing Graciella, Danielle's surrogate maternal figure. Leigh's plea with Cady to rape her and spare Danielle can be read as the culmination of her journey back to accepting Danielle as her daughter, through sparing her the damage created by male physical contact. But this could equally be Scorsese's sop to a Hollywood ending, reuniting at least some members of the family. The film stops short of suggesting a full reunification, as in the closing moments Sam literally keeps himself at arm's length, placing his hand on Leigh but not embracing her or Danielle. For her part, Leigh makes no indication she wants him any closer.

Against a lack of easy-to-identify-with characters, structures of sympathy are carefully created to ensure no intended audience support for Cady. *Cape Fear* (and the 1962 version) provides no motivation for Cady's misogyny, which works in its favour. Humanising him risks engendering audience sympathy, particularly in the remake where Sam's actions create a more complex ethical and moral framework. Therefore, despite Sam abrogating his oath to provide Cady with a full defence, the film establishes the ex-con's villainy from the outset. Initially this is through De Niro's physically imposing performance, unnerving details (e.g. the literal objectification of women in Cady's bikini-clad female-torso lighter), and references in dialogue to his past crimes.

But it is the ferocity of his attack on Lori, thirty-three minutes into the runtime, that extinguishes any potential pity for Cady. Scorsese employs his usual approach to violence in this scene, making it brief but shattering, reverberating through the remainder of the film. Electing not to show the rape, which carries dangers of unintended titillation, the film depicts the preceding sexually motivated violence. Lori's behaviour with Cady in the bar also avoids "she was asking for it" cliché, rooting her motivation in disappointment with Sam. Illeana Douglas describes how she discussed the character with Scorsese as, "[Someone] who has never done anything bad in her entire life, but one day she says, 'You know what? I'm seeing this married guy. He doesn't even care about me,' and she has this sort of self-destructive impulse…" (O'Neal, 2009).

Strick's script suggests Cady's violence and omits the cheek biting (Strick, 1990, p.33-34). That detail was a product of De Niro's research into serial sex offenders, and as Strick told me, part of the actor's quest for authenticity in the characters he portrays. This was also important for Scorsese, being "true to the society in which the film operates." In *The Making of Cape Fear*, the director speaks about depicting the stark reality the research uncovered in euphemistic legal language: "…you had these wild men out there doing horrible things and it's considered 'aggravated assault'. And one of the cases we read was just that, a man who bit part of a cheek off and he was just convicted of 'aggravated assault'. Which is an *interesting* phrase when you see the actual action. But that kind of madness I think is what we were after" (Bouzereau, 2001).

One of the most disturbing aspects of the scene, Lori laughing and unaware of the danger she is in, was input from Douglas, and a change from the scene as written in which she quickly realises Cady's intentions (Strick, 1990, p.33). Douglas also drew on the case of Jennifer Levin, a woman murdered by her boyfriend and subsequently victim-blamed for alleged promiscuity during his trial (O'Neal, 2009). Victim-blaming had recently been dramatised in *The Accused* (Kaplan, 1988), the highest profile Hollywood film of the 1980s to deal with consent and coercion. Making the victim partly culpable for their attack is also implicit in Sam's description of Cady's crime in *The Executioners*, in which both the lawyer and ex-con were servicemen at the time: "[Cady had] been pulled out [of combat] with a bad case of jungle rot and jungle nerves… It was his first trip to the city. He was drunk. She looked older, and she was out on the street at two in the morning" (MacDonald, 1957, p.5).

Fig. 16 Lori's disturbing unawareness of the danger Cady poses

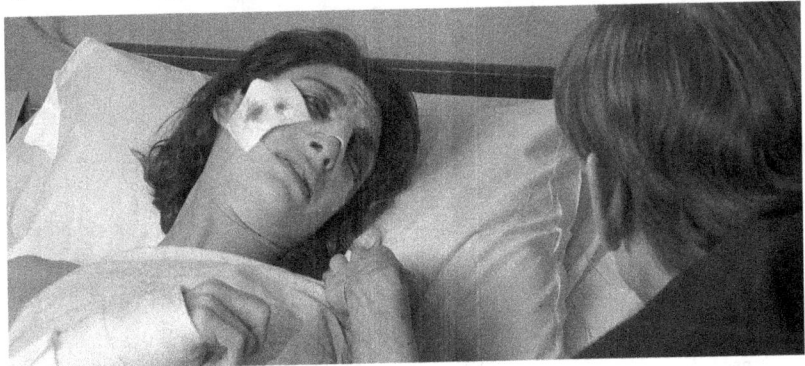

Fig. 17 Lori's post-attack terror of being victim-blamed

Cape Fear devotes a greater amount of time to the scene of Lori in the hospital post-attack than to her assault. Terrified of a legal system that positions victim-blaming as a viable weapon, Lori knows she will be placed on trial as much as Max Cady, telling Sam: "I see it every day, only this time I'm on the other side. I don't wanna explain why I was in a bar, and how much I had to drink, and what I was wearing. Not by the people I work with. Not by the guys I see cross-examining people on the stand; just *crucify* them and then laugh about it later." What Cady and Lori (and Sam) realise is that the success of Cady's revenge plan hinges on society's conspiratorial misogyny: the stigma placed upon rape survivors shields the ex-con from arrest. If Sam had not buried the evidence of Cady's victim's promiscuity, he would have presumably used it to question the veracity of her account on the witness stand. In this way, the film ensures the horror of Lori's experience and her subsequent trauma is fully recognised.

Through this structuring of sympathy, the film avoids both eroticising assault and suggesting Lori shares culpability for the attack. But does this terrorisation, no matter how brief in the run time, break the audience contract with those expecting a glossy thriller, rather than the tougher articulation of "B-grade" horror? One could argue here that Scorsese's commitment to "authenticity" was something to keep him interested while making a commercial movie. Therefore, the attack on Lori is more disturbing than the violence in yuppie horror films, which reserve the more graphic elements for the climax of act two into act three, and whose violence was never this distressing. As *Cape Fear* has not been cited for inspiring any crimes, audiences must decide whether Scorsese's treatment of the material is justified by the clearly delineated structures of sympathy.

Avoidance of pity for Cady also occurs during the climax. After placing Sam on trial, Cady laments that his lawyer could have saved him fourteen lost years. Any flickering of sympathy is immediately extinguished when he terrorises Leigh and Danielle, demanding they get on their knees and take off their clothes. But, Scorsese rejects an opportunity to make the scene more relatable for the audience. Sam, now unbound, watches impassively while his wife and daughter scream. The character's motivation is unclear; maybe he is in shock, perhaps he feels overwhelmed by a crisis for which he is partly responsible, or as Wernblad suggests, "…because Sam remains incapable, even now, of yielding his colossal narcissism" (2011, p.157)? While Sam's inaction continues the film's exploration of flawed masculinity, and keeps the climax within the Final Girl horror bracket, a more humanist director would have made him an audience proxy, depicting him displaying at least some anguish at the situation. But the suggestion that divine intervention spares Leigh and Danielle seems to have carried greater importance for Scorsese.

Whatever the motivation governing Sam's (in)actions, the scene succeeds in avoiding sympathy for Cady by making clear his violent intentions. In her excellent analysis of *Cape Fear*, Wernblad's comment that Sam is Cady's sole target, and the serial rapist attacks his family, "...*not*, as it turns out, in order to kill or harm or rape them... but to make Sam take responsibility for his actions", (2011, p.147) is the only part that sounds like wishful thinking.

Importantly, the film resists a sexualising male gaze. Women in Scorsese's movies are largely interpreted through the vantage point of the lead male. But the leads' viewpoint is often not shared by the film. In *Cape Fear*, there seems to be a deliberate decision not to present the female characters from either Sam or Cady's perspective. In the film women are typically framed in head and shoulders shots, including during scenes of rape and sexual menace. There is no full nudity or fragmentation of the female body that would invite the audience to share in Cady's excitement or rage. Lesley Stern makes a good comparison point here with De Niro's character's rape of the woman he cannot have in Sergio Leone's *Once Upon A Time in America* (1984). In that film the attack is depicted as a display of virility and the tragic act of a doomed romantic. *Cape Fear* rejects this style of presentation, portraying sexual violence solely as an act of dominance rather than foiled desire (Stern, 1995, p.216).

A typical male gaze is reserved for Cady when he is strip-searched as a means of intimidation for Sam's benefit. Through a one-way mirror, the lawyer begins watching with a smirk. Some have commented that this equates Cady in his humiliation with the film's female characters. But it plays more as a thwarting of Sam's attempts to escape the dark reflection of his past transgression, a pattern repeated throughout the film. Despite humiliating Cady through fragmenting his body in close-ups, these shots become building blocks creating an intimidating structure: the ostentatiously defined torso and muscles, the audacity of the religious tattoos inked into his skin. The dominant power of Sam and Lt. Elgart's gaze has been denied, a sentiment captured in Elgart's remark: "Gee, I don't know whether to look at him or read him."

Cady's rape while incarcerated has also been used to connect him with the film's abused women. But his comment that in prison he "learnt to get in touch with the soft, nurturing side of myself, the feminine side" can be read as him equating femininity with powerlessness. The remark is placed between Cady telling Sam that in prison he had been, "A woman; some fat, hairy hillbilly's wet dream," and his subsequent goading question on what is appropriate financial compensation for being, "…held down and sodomised by four white guys? Or four black guys? Shall my compensation be the same?"

Pam Cook writes the experience of watching horror is "about arousing the viewer's base instincts – it has nothing whatever to do with the 'uplifting' or purifying qualities of 'high' art" (1992, p.15). I would counter this by arguing horror provides the audience with a safe experience of extreme emotional responses, including fear and shock but also elation and relief. An important factor is that the audience knows going in which experience to expect. While Cady's actions are unequivocally condemned in the film, the lack of clearly defined boundaries between him and the Bowdens (particularly Sam) means aspects of his character can be found in the film's 'heroes'. This is a trope of Paranoid Horror, reflecting a character's darkness back at them. But it can generate audience unease if the expected moral distance between protagonist and antagonist is absent. A 'cleaner' depiction of *Cape Fear*'s basic narrative is found in *The Hand That Rocks the Cradle*, which gender flips the villain, reduces the sexual threat, and presents the menaced family as morally impeccable.

WE NEED TO TALK ABOUT DANNY

> Of course, you can't mention *Cape Fear* without acknowledging the breakout role for Juliette Lewis as the young daughter, which by today's standards, some of the scenes with De Niro cross the line to very disturbing. I understand for people that it's very upsetting, but it is a thriller with these moral questions underneath. – Illeana Douglas introducing *Cape Fear* on *Trailers from Hell* (2017)

In *The Making of Cape Fear* (2001), Scorsese says the film could be retold for successive generations. But decades since making that remark, there has not been an official remake and it is difficult to see how the film could now be approached without a significant overhaul, both in the general atmosphere of male-on-female sexual threat, and particularly in depicting Cady's violation of Danielle.

An indicator of the cultural conversation shifting in thirty years is how little contemporary commentary existed on *Cape Fear* featuring an antagonist targeting an adolescent minor. While the film does not condone or celebrate Cady's exploitation of Danielle's nascent sexuality, it is hard to imagine Hollywood today producing a film with this subject matter in such a style. A scene in which Cady, pretending to be her new drama teacher, charms Danielle over the phone, depicts the girl with one dropped shoulder strap. Understandable, perhaps, as cinematic shorthand indicating the ex-con is manipulating her adolescent confusion and naivete, this also demonstrates how *Cape Fear*'s articulation of its themes resides in a previous era. Of the film's shots featuring female characters this one verges most on the male-gaze, but is counterbalanced by a consciously created atmosphere of dread at Cady's deception.

Scorsese follows Wesley Strick's script in having Danielle's narration open and close the film as her "reminiscence". Beginning on a close-up of Danielle, we realise she is standing in front of a chalkboard, delivering the homework she mentions later in the film, which makes us curious to see an alternate version of *Cape Fear*, ending on a reaction shot of stunned classmates as she concludes her story.

Choosing Danielle as narrator, writes Cook, suggests she conjures Cady as a defence against "her incestuous desire for Sam", and "'employs' him to violate her mother" (1992, p.15). While Danielle rejects her parents until Cady's murder of Graciella, the film does not fully bear out this reading. Rather, Danielle is cast as an unwitting accomplice in Cady's plan until she realises her corruptor's true intent. In her study of *Taxi Driver*, Amy Taubin suggests a position between these two points, writing, "*Cape Fear* is a much more interesting film when it's read through the young girl's subjectivity – as a narrative of female sexuality and coming to power" (2000, p.66). This is a more hopeful reading, locating Danielle as the film's protagonist. The story can be interpreted as Danielle's empowerment, conquering a patriarchy embodied in the tyrannical Cady and the self-serving, disingenuous Sam. The character is given enough screen time and plot incident to establish an arc that supports this, and Lewis' nuanced performance develops Danielle as if she is playing the lead. Salvation for the family also comes from the daughter, who closes the film with the statement that she would rather live, even if future problems *may* stem from how she behaves with her own family, remaining true to the film's Gothic and religious motifs of past sins being visited upon the children. But,

Scorsese does not seem interested in Danielle for this. Her role is what she can reveal about Cady, his conflict with Sam, and a world of male toxicity, meaning *Cape Fear* again emerges as an incoherent text, wrestling with multiple viewpoints all battling for attention.

In the school theatre scene, Cady's behaviour echoes that of Harvey Keitel's pimp Sport in *Taxi Driver*, duplicitously flattering Jodie Foster's Iris. Both feature an antagonist manipulating a child for his own benefit, financial gain in the case of Sport. Both scenes present unguarded femininity as something that will be abused in a world of noxious masculinity. The theatre sequence is also more in keeping with Scorsese's previous output than the chase scene featuring Cady and Danielle that was originally scripted, lifted from the 1962 original. But, the idea originated with Wesley Strick, who told me Scorsese so hated the chase that the writer elected to go for an exact opposite, "a seduction". The completed scene was a combination of Strick's original script, plus cast and director improvisation sessions incorporated into subsequent rewrites.

While the scene is presented as an act of transgression and corruption, not constructed in a way to encourage identification with Cady's satisfaction, its method of production resides in a less cautious time of Hollywood filmmaking. Namely, the moment when Cady twice slips his thumb into Danielle's mouth before kissing her, an action not in the script and which the 17-year-old Juliette Lewis was unaware would happen. De Niro had told Scorsese what he was going to do, but the director did not tell Lewis because, "Marty wanted that look of surprise from her" (Strick interview with author). Lewis herself has never spoken out against the manner in which the scene was shot, and in the 2001 making-of documentary described the moment as "...really incredible to shoot," adding, "...after that I was so exhilarated because artistically there was such an energy and exchange" (Bouzereau, 2001). At the time this was regarded as an acceptable method to elicit the best performance, Strick telling me, "It would not fly today, but in terms of filmmaking technique then we didn't think that was uncool." On this point, it is the sexual politics behind the filmmaking practices themselves that belong to a different era.

FINAL THOUGHTS

The controversy over *Cape Fear*'s sexual politics cannot be settled here. While to me the film does not invite the audience to enjoy the terrorisation of its female characters, a final point on its shortcomings can be made in comparing it to *The Silence of the Lambs*, released earlier the same year. Groundbreaking at the time for placing a woman in the traditionally male cinematic role of investigator, a contemporary *Sight and Sound* article by Amy Taubin declared it, "…a profoundly feminist movie… It takes a familiar narrative and shakes up the gender and sexuality stuff. It's a slasher film in which the woman is the hero rather than victim…" (May 1991, p.18). All accurate, although Demme's film also received criticism, at time of release and in the years since, for perceived transphobia and homophobia. This comparison to *The Silence of the Lambs* is valuable because it highlights indifference to female agency as a possible form of misogyny. Are *Cape Fear*'s structures of sympathy, avoidance of titillation in depicting sexual threat, and casting of women who will develop their own roles sufficient counterbalance to Scorsese's use of female characters solely to reflect male psychologies?

Balanced representation between the sexes is not part of his job description, of course. At a press conference for *The Irishman*, the director grew frustrated with a question about the lack of female representation in his films, replying, "Am I supposed to?... If the story doesn't call for it… it's a waste of everybody's time. If the story calls for a female character lead, why not?" (Anderson, 2019). What is not said here is what may ultimately save Scorsese from having to repeatedly answer this question: he is not interested in depicting a female point of view. Staying "true to the society in which the film operates" may not hold as much weight as first appears when spoken by a director who can choose his own projects. In Scorsese's cinema, the horrors not only lie in Hell, but in an absence of God. This can correlate to a director not hating his female characters, but being less interested in them. Whether this equates to misogyny is a question for further debate.

There is value too in reviewing how subsequent films have tackled similar subject matter. David Slade's *Hard Candy* (2005) can be viewed as a next iteration of the sexual politics in *Cape Fear*. In a film that trades on *Little Red Riding Hood* imagery and tropes, the fourteen-year-old Hayley (Elliot Page) is targeted by charismatic older man Jeff (Patrick Wilson). Here, however, Jeff is the real mark, terrorised and put on trial in his house by a teen who knows what he plans to do, and what he has already done. *Hard Candy* therefore emerges as a power inversion of *Cape Fear*'s school theatre scene. Themes of sexual violence, burgeoning sexuality, the commodification of adolescence, and revenge vs. justice all play out in a tense two-hander that shifts from indie drama to thriller to horror. Memorable again is the teenage actor's performance, but here 'defanging' the wolf in various ways rather than being charmed by him. That Page came out as transgender in 2020 has added a further, meta-level of gender commentary to the film.

Recent rape-revenge films from female voices have demonstrated how the narrative trend can address issues of power and coercion in the twenty-first-century. The Soska Sisters' pre-#MeToo *American Mary* (2012) uses the theme of body modification as a path to liberation. Medical student and rape survivor Mary (Katherine Isabelle) does not modify her own physique, but through radical surgery turns male aggressors into bodies she can control, mirroring what they did to her. Sophia Takal's *Black Christmas* (2019) approaches the rape-revenge plot from a standpoint that retribution brings no peace. As Lena Wilson writes in an article on rape-revenge cinema, the characters here and in similar stories are not condemned to a quest for vengeance: "They find a peace that ultimately matters more than confrontations with their attackers" (Wilson, 2021). Jennifer Kent's *The Nightingale* (2018) is another film that ultimately adopts this viewpoint. Emerald Fennell's *Promising Young Woman* (2020), about which Wilson has reservations, is more jaundiced in its view of life post-rape, even for those not directly attacked. Nonetheless, in darkly ironic fashion it says women will make their voice heard, no matter how violent the men's attempts to silence them.

Bar period piece *The Nightingale*, these films, plus the TV series *I May Destroy You* (2020), shift women out of gendered roles. The protagonists of *American Mary* and *Promising Young Woman* are, or were, medical students, the women in *Black Christmas* attend a prestigious college that will presumably lead to successful careers, and Michaela Cole is a hard-living author in *I May Destroy You*. Placed beside *The Silence of the Lambs* and these more recent titles, the feminine gendered roles in *Cape Fear* leave little doubt as to which characters hold Scorsese's attention. Another point of difference between the film and the most recent movies mentioned is in using sexual threat as one plot device within a wider narrative. But, as previously mentioned, views on the (in)appropriateness of this lie with the individual viewer.

Chapter 4: Filmmaking at the Speed of Fear

While Steven Spielberg's company may have co-produced, there is nothing amblin' about *Cape Fear*. Scorsese takes the kineticism of Henry Hill's final cocaine-fuelled day as a gangster in *Goodfellas* and uses it here to create a state of near-permanent panic.

Slow motion, one of the director's most deployed techniques throughout his career, is notable by its scarcity. He often uses it to make a character point or convey the surreality of a violent moment: Jimmy Burke smoking a cigarette and ruminating on killing Morrie in *Goodfellas*, Sugar Ray Robinson swelling to monstrous proportions before beating Jake La Motta to a pulp in *Raging Bull*. But in *Cape Fear*, slow motion's chief function is to ensure audience clarity either before or during scenes of mayhem: a shot of the houseboat's anchor being dropped into the river, Kersek's gun arcing through the air during the climactic struggle, Sam attempting to bring a giant rock down on Cady's head. An exception is the subtle use of slow motion when Leigh rises from the swampy riverbank during the film's final minutes. This moment is also shot in reverse to add an extra layer of subliminal unease, a technique Scorsese would revisit in *Bringing Out the Dead* (see Chapter 5 for a discussion of this film).

The bombastic visual style captures both Sam's anxiety and Cady's unstoppable momentum. The film's style is soaked in the drive of its antagonist: shots move with inexorable speed and the sound design is amped way up, particularly during scene transitions, allowing little time for the audience to take a breath. An early indication that Cady has mastery over *Cape Fear*'s form is when he marches directly into the camera when leaving prison. Other examples include his silhouette blocking the screen during the Bowdens' cinema outing, and a 180° camera rotation so the ex-con, suspended upside down in his apartment, seems to reverse gravity and appear the right way up. Conversely, Sam is photographed as if under scrutiny, frequently caught in uncomfortable close-up, framed from elevated angles.

Breaking down the film to its component parts, *Cape Fear* contains c.1,455 shots. Excluding end credits but including the opening Universal logo as it features diegetic thunder and rain sound effects, on an internet streaming service the film runs 118

Fig. 18 Cady's inversion of gravity demonstrates his control over the film's form

minutes and 36 seconds. This gives it an average-shot-length (ASL) of 4.9 seconds. By comparison, *Goodfellas* has an ASL of approximately 6.7 seconds (Bordwell, 2006). In the twenty-first century, Scorsese would follow the filmmaking trend of faster editing, with his Oscar winning *The Departed* having an ASL of 2.7 seconds (Bordwell, 2006). But tempo of editing is not the only method by which Scorsese conveys narrative velocity. As effective is the audacious camerawork, which led Stuart Klawans in his review for *The Nation* to remark that the film's biggest stars are "…Martin Scorsese and his Wonder Camera" (Klawans, 1991). A still composition is a rare beast in *Cape Fear*, with shots frequently reframing from wider perspectives and higher angles to a narrower view, often resting on characters' faces. With an ASL of under 5 seconds, this strengthens the impression of a film constantly in movement.

Sometimes cuts will be disguised in whip pans, as when Sam's PA tells him Leigh is on the phone, after Cady has killed the dog. A clever effect to heighten tension is that the second whip pan ends on a closer shot of Sam's PA than the first time we see her, despite the scene resembling a single take. Staying in Sam's office, another memorable display of scene blocking is when he calls Lee Heller to retain his services, only to discover Cady has beaten him to the punch. Across 32 seconds, the camera drops from an overhead medium close-up on Sam, follows him pacing his office, then alternates between medium wide and medium close-up, finally placing on a tight close-up of Sam as Heller tells him he has been retained by Cady. Unusual angles and continuous movement of a character within an increasingly claustrophobic shot once again generates an atmosphere of anxiety. Overhead framing conveys a God's-eye-view of the action, suggesting a higher power is observing events unfold. Other God's-eye-view examples appear throughout, particularly around moments of violence, including Cady on the bed with Lori, when Cady is attacked by the hired goons, or when Kersek is killed. This culminates in numerous overhead shots during the climax, of both the houseboat battered on stormy waters and the struggle inside.

While sharing some crossover with what was happening in slasher cinema, the film does not employ POV in traditional slasher manner. This is partly because there is no need to disguise Cady's identity until a final act reveal, and because Scorsese would have presumably balked at the notion he was making a film that could be compared to the stalk-and-slash movies that had proliferated during the 1980s. In Cape Fear the director plays fast and loose with POV shots, sharing them amongst different characters. As Danielle approaches the school theatre, there looks to be a shot of the basement hallway from her perspective. In the scene when Cady is assaulted, we see his headbutt from the point-of-view of the headbutted character. During the climax, there is an unmistakable point-of-view moment from Cady's perspective, his hand in shot holding a gun as he looks for Sam. Later, the lawyer will have his own POV moment when regarding the blood on his hands before washing them in the river. This final example links to Scorsese's most ostentatious stylistic decision: Cady breaking the fourth wall and speaking directly to the God's-eye-view camera during Sam's 'trial' on the houseboat. The implication is that we the audience have adopted the perspective of the higher power sitting in judgement. Moments after this, Cady orders Leigh and Danielle to strip. But his plan is ruined by the houseboat hitting rocks in the river, the film responding to our wish that the female characters be spared.

As interesting are the moments that resemble POV shots but are never anchored to a character. Many are suggested to be from Cady's perspective, but are never confirmed as such: a fixed view on the Bowden residence at night, a tracking shot through trees finally resting on the houseboat. Again, the antagonist seems to be bending the film's form to his will. Alongside this menace, Scorsese uses the device to imply supernatural abilities in his villain. During the sequence when Kersek and Sam wait for Cady to invade the Bowden home, a prowling shot glides through the garden alongside the house. Long enough in duration for the audience to assume it is the ex-con's POV, the shot then

Fig. 19 A God's-eye-view shot as Cady breaks the fourth wall

cranes upwards to Danielle's window on the second floor. If this is a POV shot, then it is from the perspective of a character who has just taken flight.

Another device employed to keep audiences off-kilter is beginning scenes on a close-up. Examples here include a rebounding ball during a squash game, a canted overhead shot of an Evian bottle when Cady charms Lori at the bar, a piano hammer hitting empty space where the wire should be after he attacks her, and in the courtroom scene, a cassette recorder playing Sam's threat to harm his nemesis. With the audience off balance, zooms and fast dollies are then used to intensify the impact of the violence. Cady punching an offscreen Lori is given added shocking momentum by the low angle zoom past him as he lands the blow. During the climax, flash zooms into Leigh and Danielle either before or after Sam is pistol whipped by Cady enhance the effect. A zoom in to Danielle bolting upright in bed from a nightmare recalls the shot in *Goodfellas* when Henry Hill snorts cocaine to keep pace with a particularly hectic day. All these elements combine for the sole purpose of keeping the heart rate elevated.

The 'panic-above-suspense' approach has its detractors. Tom Shone writes that on *Cape Fear* Scorsese is "...a hot-head who cannot wait to bring everyone else to the boil", going on to say: "*Cape Fear* is that weirdest of creatures: a thriller plugged into the nerve endings, not of its audience, but its director, who can't get out of his own way..." (2014, p.157-8). Undoubtedly the filmmaker lacks the detachment which enabled Hitchcock to create multiple masterpiece suspense sequences. Championed for putting his heart and soul into every movie, Scorsese was never going to stop himself from diving into the characters' moral morass. Remember, here is a director who when talking about the audience admits, "I *do* want them to see the way I see" (in Thompson/Christie, 1996, p.88). But this again highlights how restrictive is the 'thriller' label when discussing *Cape Fear*, and may explain the director's dissatisfaction with the film if he believes he delivered a thriller. Horror is a genre that comfortably accommodates the aesthetic and thematic excesses Scorsese deemed necessary, and it is genuinely exciting to see what he does with a style more reminiscent of Sam Raimi or Dario Argento.

But, in the two moments of purest dread – Cady picking up Lori in the bar, and his violation of Danielle in the school theatre – Scorsese pares back the style, favouring simple set ups, with any reframing motivated only by character movement. As both scenes are formally lo-fi, one feeds into the other; the tempo of the scene with Lori is subliminally felt in the later scene with Danielle. The savage end to Lori's encounter with Cady instills a dread about what will happen to the Bowden teenager. The thumb-sucking and deep kiss is unexpected and an abuse of a different kind, doubling as an attack on Sam, with his daughter now pitted against him.

Assisting in the creation of these visuals was veteran cinematographer and director Freddie Francis. The London born Francis was himself no stranger to depicting a domestic crisis in a Gothic style, having photographed *The Innocents* for director Jack Clayton. He also brought a Gothic touch to films he directed, including *Nightmare* (1964), about a girl plagued by fears she has inherited her mother's murderous insanity, and *Mumsy, Nanny, Sonny & Girly* (1970), another 'mad mum' movie, with the matriarch here ordering her psychotic children to abduct potential father figures. Francis was also familiar with the 2.39:1 aspect ratio that Scorsese was using for the first time, along with even wider formats, *The Innocents* being shot in true 2.66:1 CinemaScope. As with that 1961 chiller, on *Cape Fear* Francis would employ strong lights to capture images in striking deep focus, allowing little opportunity for characters to hide. Rather than the peek-a-boo shocks of John Carpenter's *Halloween*, this widescreen overwhelms and ensnares characters, typically through vivid close-ups or exaggerated angles. Some of the most flamboyant shots are courtesy of the cinematographer introducing his director to the Panatate, a camera rig that allowed for the 180° rotation in Cady's apartment, plus 360° rotations to convey the houseboat's destruction during the climax. With *Cape Fear*, the CinemaScope of Nicholas Ray's *Bigger Than Life* (1956) is fused with the Panavision of *The Entity*.

Complementing the visuals is Elmer Bernstein's reorchestration of Bernard Herrmann's score for the 1962 movie. Bernstein worked through 49 cues for the film, his layered rearrangements generating a sense of dread where Herrmann's cues worked on brute shock, an aural complement to Mitchum's barrel-chested brutality. A comparison listen to the title track demonstrates how Bernstein reimagined Herrmann's work for a 1990s film. As a 1992 *Empire* article elucidates, "Rising chords played on wind instruments, instead *descend*, as if the weight of the Bowdens' situation is sucking them down into the mire, represented by swirling, nervous violins" (Morgan, 1992, p.65). Of course, the swampy mire is where Cady dwells in the abstract opening credits, suggesting the antagonist inhabits the soundtrack as much as the visuals. Compounding this is the score's use of the tritone, the so-called 'devil's interval', spanning three notes between B and F, and banned by the Catholic Church in the Middle Ages (Wernblad, 2011, p.149).

Scorsese's vision meant losing certain cues from Herrmann's original score. 'The House', a breezy flute and strings arrangement that introduces 1962's blissful Bowdens, has no place in 1991's quagmire of dysfunction. Instead, Scorsese would add a sense of unease to Danielle and Leigh's introductory scene by setting it to a low-key reorchestration of a segment from the main title cue. In *The Making of Cape Fear*, Bernstein described how the original score had nothing to match the remake's thunderous finale. The solution was to utilise music from Bernard Herrmann's unused score for *Torn Curtain* (Bouzereau, 2001). This score, rejected by Alfred Hitchcock in a move that ended his relationship with Herrmann, provided the requisite timpani and horns bombast for the climactic reckoning. Specifically a track entitled 'The Killing', rearranged for two cues in the remake, 'The Fight' and 'Destruction'. 'The Fight' also incorporated elements from another *Torn Curtain* track, 'Hotel Berlin'.

Herrmann's music had often been set to Saul Bass' title designs, most famously in Hitchcock movies such as *Psycho* and *Vertigo* (1958). Although Bass did not provide titles for the 1962 version of *Cape Fear*, Scorsese recruited him and his wife Elaine to create "…a mini-movie that precedes the picture" (Bouzereau, 2001). As previously mentioned, they and the director viewed the opening sequence as evoking a "…notion of monsters from the deep". Thus, Cady pervades the film from the first second, with even the Universal logo accompanied by the sound of rain and thunder, then shimmering as if beneath the Cape Fear river. The character continues to be subtly invoked throughout the opening credits. Wernblad remarks how an eagle, in Christianity symbolising a Heaven-sent messenger, appears under Robert De Niro's name. As the end credits finish their roll, a sound of beating wings is heard, implying a return heavenwards (Wernblad, 2011, p.149). We have previously commented upon the religious significance of the silhouette with the prominent left hand.

Beyond this religious symbolism, and the religious connotations of water and baptism, the opening credits establish a horror film atmosphere. The cast and crew text echoes the font used in *Psycho*'s credits, caught 'mid-jag'. A close-up of an eye, wide in terror, follows the title credit, and disturbing figures emerge from the murk. Foreshadowing Cady's attack on Lori and the thumb-sucking violation of Danielle, a large, open mouth fades in and out. Over Scorsese's director credit, a tear, or a blood droplet, or possibly a bloody tear, washes the screen red. As Bernstein revisited mothballed Herrmann music for the score, the Basses went to their archive of unused footage for this sequence. The eyeball, mouth and other unsettling shots were photographed for, but never incorporated into, the credits of John Frankenheimer's 1966 sci-fi chiller *Seconds* (Bouzereau, 2001), another film featuring a character looking to escape his unsatisfying life, but instead discovering the high cost of change. The Basses were also responsible for a sly suggestion of the supernatural in a shot that begins the film's final segment. When shimmering waters calm to reveal the reflection of a road sign, the words 'Cape Fear' are not reversed…

None of this would exist without Wesley Strick's script. A former rock music critic, Strick had demonstrated a flair for genre-blending as co-writer of *Arachnophobia* (Marshall, 1990). This comedy-horror also threatened an upwardly mobile family with a foe uncannily able to be everywhere at once. When interviewing Strick he spoke highly of Nick Nolte, an actor often overlooked in discussions of *Cape Fear*, despite being the ostensible lead. Describing Nolte as "a really good soldier", Strick said how he expected the actor to "explode with frustration because he plays a character who is continually thwarted", and is denied a final hero moment. "But he never did… I have to hand that to him; he just took the abuse that we dished out to him in almost every scene of the movie" (interview with author). That the screen character of Sam Bowden plays second fiddle to Max Cady is something Gregory Peck understood back on the first film. Speaking in *The Making of Cape Fear* (1962), Peck recounts telling J. Lee Thompson, "… my part is not really the lead. The lead is Cady the villain, so whoever plays that will steal the picture from me" (Bouzereau, 2001).

An unusual choice for the film, Nolte speaks to the moral murk Scorsese wanted for the character of Sam. The director discussed the role with Robert Redford, contrasting his "wholesomeness" with the malevolence De Niro was going to bring. "But ultimately we didn't need that kind of symbolism in the casting" (Thompson/Christie, 1996, p.165). However, Nolte was not immediately at the forefront of Scorsese's mind, the director still thinking of him in terms of the bearish, drunken painter he had played in the *Life Lessons* segment of *New York Stories*. Only after seeing him slimmed down and spruced up at a Museum of Modern Art screening of *Goodfellas* did Scorsese say to De Niro, "Look, that's our lawyer" (Thompson/Christie, 1996, p.166).

Cape Fear marked the director's first experience with optical effects. Digital effects company Illusion Arts allowed Scorsese to play God, Freddie Francis recalling the director being presented with various dramatic cloud formations and asked, "Which sky do you want?" (Morgan, 1991b). Small wonder he chose roiling skies, evoking memories of Norman in front of the Bates mansion against a similarly troubled firmament in *Psycho*, or the angry clouds churning above Hill House in *The Haunting*, Scorsese's no.1 film in that scariest of all-time list. One cleverly disguised optical effect is how the film makes Robert De Niro more imposing than Nick Nolte, despite standing three inches shorter and being of slighter build. In their scenes together, one actor is typically sitting or kneeling while the other stands, or they are separated as with the one-way mirror during the strip search. At De Niro's request, scenes displaying his torso were filmed late in production, so the actor was at peak physical condition.

Scorsese viewed the climactic set-piece, involving a full-scale houseboat set on hydraulic mounts, as an opportunity to use hitherto untested directorial muscles. Illeana Douglas recalls Steven Spielberg being brought in at Scorsese's request to assist with this action-heavy climax. Douglas calls Spielberg's input "…instrumental in helping out the dramatic tension toward the end of the movie, which Marty really felt was not his strong suit and Spielberg was really good at" (Douglas, 2017). Thus, the remake's original director literally came aboard to imbue the film with some of his style. Editor Thelma Schoonmaker explained how they were required to assemble the climax first, allowing the team in the UK to match that footage with the houseboat miniatures they were shooting (Morgan, 1991d). Schoonmaker would also say the storytelling rigours of the genre were a challenge for her director, who in the past could place plot second to character (Morgan, 1991d). But the large scale denouement successfully marries theme, character and an audience expectation for a hyperbolic climax. An understandable expectation: after transforming Cady into a villain of Satanic proportions, the riverbank tussle that ended the original film would have been thin gruel indeed.

After reshoots to help with audience comprehension of events during the climax, *Cape Fear* was completed and released. What happened next is the focus for our final chapter.

Chapter 5: Legacy and Impact

But really I don't want to do remakes. – Martin Scorsese (quoted in Thompson/Christie, 1996, p.106)

Cape Fear was released to divided critical opinion but enthusiastic box office, delivering Scorsese his highest grossing movie up to that point. Critical response from some quarters was ecstatic. Elsewhere, along with accusations of misogyny, some critics saw Scorsese selling himself short, even when impressed with the film. Roger Ebert declared, "Most directors would distinguish themselves by making a film this good. From the man who made *Taxi Driver*, *Raging Bull*, *After Hours*, and *Goodfellas*, this is not an advance" (quoted in Ebert, 2008, p.131).

Others were more appreciative. Barry Norman featured it in the *Film '92* 'Films of the Year' show, commenting, "Even Martin Scorsese got up a lot of people's noses with an out-and-out commercial movie, *Cape Fear*, a brilliant, violent remake… condemned as 'dangerous' and 'morally bankrupt'. In fact, it's neither of those things; it's simply a cracking good picture" (Norman, 1992). Although Norman did call the film's "slam-bang Hollywood ending" its "weakness", again, when viewed through the expectations of horror cinema the finale is a satisfying culmination of the film's themes, particularly all roads leading home no matter how far characters flee.

In the US, some cinemagoers were physically overwhelmed by the experience of watching *Cape Fear*. Strick told me, "I did hear stories about people having to leave the movie for a breath of fresh air, and then fainting in the lobby. I was a rock journalist in the seventies, and at a Bay City Rollers concert saw kids being taken into the lobby and lain out on the carpet. Fifteen years later it was happening with *Cape Fear*. Which we didn't expect, but it made for good publicity" (interview with author).

The film performed respectably on the awards circuit, although struggled to convert nominations into actual wins. Robert De Niro and Juliette Lewis received most attention, in the Best Actor and Best Supporting Actress categories. At the Academy Awards, De Niro lost out to Anthony Hopkins for *The Silence of the Lambs*, and Lewis to Mercedes Ruehl for *The Fisher King* (Gilliam, 1991). At the BAFTA Awards, Freddie Francis and Thelma Schoonmaker were nominated for Best Cinematography and Best

Editing. They lost to Dante Spinotti for *The Last of the Mohicans* (Mann, 1992) and Joe Hutshing and Pietro Scalia for *JFK* (Stone, 1991) respectively. The Berlin International Film Festival placed *Cape Fear* in competition for its highest award, the Golden Berlin Bear. Ultimately, yuppie horror was defeated by Lawrence Kasdan's yuppie sympathetic *Grand Canyon* (1991).

An indication of the film's thirty-year-old status is Robert De Niro and Juliette Lewis' 'Best Kiss' nomination at the 1992 MTV Movie + TV Awards. It lost to the pre-pubescent pairing of Anna Chlumsky and Macaulay Culkin in *My Girl* (Zieff, 1991). At the same ceremony, De Niro would miss out on a Best Actor award to Arnold Schwarzenegger for *Terminator 2: Judgment Day* (Cameron, 1991), and Best Villain to Rebecca De Mornay in *The Hand That Rocks the Cradle*. As mentioned, the latter movie can be viewed as a female-led telling of a scenario similar to *Cape Fear*. That film avoided controversy and, with an $88m domestic haul, proved more palatable than Scorsese's movie, which drew $79m (although *The Hand That Rocks the Cradle*'s worldwide gross of $140m fell short of *Cape Fear*'s $182m).

That *The Simpsons* (1989-) dedicated an entire episode to parodying *Cape Fear*'s plot is an indication of the film's impact upon release. 'Cape Feare' (S05, E02) aired in the US on 7th October 1993 and would receive an Emmy nomination for its reworking of Bernard Herrmann's original score. The episode also parodied *Psycho*, plus *The Night of the Hunter*, with 'LUV' and 'HĀT' tattooed on villain Sideshow Bob's three-fingered hands. In 2019, *Time* magazine ranked it no.9 in a top 10 best *Simpsons* episodes. The episode would itself be given a postmodern spin in Anne Washburn's 2012 play, *Mr. Burns, a Post-Electric Play*. Here, survivors of an apocalyptic event gather to recount the 'Cape Feare' episode. In the play's new society *The Simpsons* becomes a familiar myth, and the repurposing of art from previous eras to comment on current events repeats all over again. Another comedy institution, *Seinfeld* (1989-1998), referenced the film in the episode 'The Bookstore' (S09, E07), which aired 9th April 1998. After Jerry has ratted out Uncle Leo for shoplifting, Leo takes the form of Max Cady in Jerry's nightmares. The film has also been referenced in *Rick and Morty* (2013-), *It's Always Sunny in Philadelphia* (2005-), *South Park* (1997-), and *Cobra Kai* (2018-).

In 2014, heavily tattooed adult movie actor Bonnie Rotten directed the gender-flipped porn parody *Cape Fear XXX*, in which she also starred as Maxine Cady. As much as budget allowed it was faithful to the plot of Scorsese's film, but aged-up the character of Dani to college student. Here Cady has also been imprisoned for the rape of a woman, but an exploration of same-sex sexual violence is beyond the remit the film provides itself. Despite Maxine Cady's villainy, Rotten's myriad tattoos are a reminder of how attitudes towards inked skin have shifted in thirty years, away from typically denoting criminality and becoming more a form of self-expression. *Cape Fear XXX* was nominated in six categories at the 2015 Adult Video News Awards, including Best Actress and Best Director (Parody) for Rotten. The performer said she made the film because, "I really love Robert De Niro, and I thought this is a really great movie that he did, and he's such a creep and so crazy in it" (Kernes, 2014, p.42).

Max Cady was part of a trend of insane geniuses in films during the 1990s. An early example was Kathryn Bigelow's feminist reworking of the cop movie, *Blue Steel* (1990), with Ron Silver's psychopathic Wall Street broker playing lethal games with Jamie Lee Curtis' rookie officer. Hannibal Lecter would become the most enduring villain from this wave, Hopkins' performance in *The Silence of the Lambs* capturing the public's imagination, transforming the insane shrink into a horror icon. Upon *Cape Fear*'s release, Cady's cannibalism seemed on brand for larger-than-life movie villains due to Lecter's culinary proclivities. Kersek's comment to Sam that an inmate who hated Cady was found with a broken neck and "tongue bit off" reminds us of Clarice Starling being told Lecter calmly consumed a nurse's tongue after feigning chest pains. A scene deleted from *Cape Fear* would have taken the Lecter connection further. Sharp-eyed audiences will notice that Kersek is wearing Cady's shirt when Sam and Leigh find him dead in the kitchen. Reminiscent of Lecter's wardrobe-change jailbreak, Leigh realises Cady dressed Kersek in his blue and white striped shirt after killing the private eye, so the police would think Sam shot Kersek after mistaking him for the ex-con. Lecter's psychotic brilliance and Cady's fundamentalist drive would combine in the character of John Doe in David Fincher's *Seven*. Lecter, Cady and Doe can be viewed as a triumvirate of insane teachers, each of them targeting someone they believe requires instruction.

De Niro would channel Max Cady into three more films he made during the 1990s. These bevelled Cady's rough edges and diluted the murky moral waters explored by Scorsese. In Michael Caton-Jones' enjoyable *This Boy's Life* (1993), Leonardo DiCaprio is menaced by De Niro's abusive, under-educated stepfather, a man whose sexual dysfunction means he refuses to allow wife Ellen Burstyn to see his face during coitus. A year later there was Kenneth Branagh's agreeably overblown adaptation of *Frankenstein*. Cady's relentless drive was less successfully brought to Tony Scott's forgettable *The Fan* (1996). This tale of De Niro's baseball obsessive targeting Wesley Snipes' star player fell flat, and would have benefitted from less *Cape Fear* influence and more *The King of Comedy*.

Other *Cape Fear* alumni would find career highlights in cinema and television of the fantastic. Wesley Strick revisited one of the great horror icons in Mike Nichols' *Wolf* (1994), in which Jack Nicholson's mild-mannered publishing professional is given a new lease of life through lycanthropy. The words of Om Puri's doctor in the film bring Cady to mind, but also Sam before his fall: "It feels good to be a wolf, doesn't it? Power without guilt. Love without doubt." Unfortunately, Strick would have less luck updating horror icon Freddy Krueger for the little-loved remake of *A Nightmare on Elm Street* (Bayer, 2010). A year after *Cape Fear*, Strick was post-Freudian again with *Final Analysis* (Joanou, 1992), a love triangle thriller with Richard Gere as a psychiatrist out of his depth with gangster's wife Kim Basinger. The writer kept it in the (dysfunctional) family into the new millennium. *The Glass House* (Sackheim, 2001) was an unusual psycho thriller, with Leelee Sobieski wary of her 'perfect' foster parents. *Hitched* (2001), which Strick also directed, saw Sheryl Lee holding hostage philandering husband Anthony Michael Hall in their soundproof basement.

Jessica Lange would win two Primetime Emmys playing different characters in *American Horror Story* (2011–). This pastiche series refracts various horror sub-genres, from haunted houses to devil cults to slasher flicks, through a postmodern queer-feminist lens. Nick Nolte made for a memorable monster in Oliver Stone's *U-Turn* (1997). Possibly the ripest example of Southern Gothic turned out by a Hollywood studio in the past thirty years, it is a film whose depiction of familial dysfunction leaves *Cape Fear* becalmed on the river. Nolte portrays a fearsome patriarch targeted for murder by his abused wife/daughter Jennifer Lopez, Sean Penn playing the hapless foil entangled in her scheme.

Juliette Lewis moved to the wrong side of the law for a brace of controversial Charles Starkweather and Caril Ann Fugate-inspired serial killer movies. Starkweather and

Fugate's random 1957-58 killing spree had previously been the inspiration for Terrence Malick's *Badlands* (1973). Dominic Sena's *Kalifornia* (1993) paired her with Brad Pitt, the murderous duo embarking upon a road trip with journalist David Duchovny and his photographer girlfriend Michelle Forbes. The outrage that greeted Oliver Stone's *Natural Born Killers* (1994) eclipsed even that of *Cape Fear*. The film was accused of inspiring copycat killings, and author John Grisham supported a case brought against the filmmakers for culpability in one particular murder. Loosely based on a Quentin Tarantino script, Stone's film also featured a murderous couple (Lewis and Woody Harrelson) being tailed by a journalist (Robert Downey, Jr.). After killing her sexually abusive father and cowed mother, the pair take a homicidal road trip that transforms them into ironic superstars. Predicting the rise of 'anything to be famous' reality TV, *Natural Born Killers*' channel-hopping visual and audio design also prophesied post-narrative mash-up media.

Lewis would team up with Tarantino for Robert Rodriguez's vampire-action movie *From Dusk Till Dawn* (1996). Wearing its postmodernist cine-literacy on its bloodied sleeve, the film begins as *Natural Born Killers* before becoming *The Evil Dead* (Raimi, 1981) meets *Assault on Precinct 13* (Carpenter, 1976). The actor would also appear in Kathryn Bigelow's sci-fi serial killer shocker *Strange Days* (1995), about a VR technology that allows people to record memories and sensations others can then experience on playback. A rape scene features a woman experiencing her rapist's excitement when he plugs his headset into hers. An end of the century take on *Peeping Tom*'s themes of scopophilia, insanity and spectator culpability, like *Cape Fear*, *Strange Days* was met with both praise and condemnation.

SCORSESE AND HORROR AFTER *CAPE FEAR*

There is an irony in Martin Scorsese saying he did not want to do remakes. They have been good to him. When discussing *Cape Fear*'s financial success at the time of *Kundun* (1997), he said, "...it gave me *The Age of Innocence*, it gave me this picture, (*Cape Fear*) did a lot" (Taubin, 1998, p.9). In the same interview, however, he expressed frustration with mainstream Hollywood filmmaking, declaring, "I don't want to make movies like *Cape Fear* anymore that stick to a conventional plot. I'm getting bored, I don't like working for someone else. Doing someone else's movie is a hard job" (Taubin, 1998, p.9).

But, 2006's *The Departed*, Scorsese's remake of Andrew Lau and Alan Mak's 2002 Hong Kong thriller *Infernal Affairs*, is conventionally plotted, *was* made at the behest of Warner Bros. *and* nabbed Scorsese an overdue Best Director Academy Award. The film also won Best Adapted Screenplay for William Monahan, Best Editing for Thelma Schoonmaker, and Best Picture, the only Scorsese film to do so as of this writing. *The Departed* shares an oddly large amount of connective tissue with his first remake. It was the director's first film to be set in the present day since *Cape Fear*. Both films provided a financial fillip that rescued him from the personal debt of a passion project: *Cape Fear* put him back in the black after *The Last Temptation of Christ*, and *The Departed* did the same after *Gangs of New York* (Schickel, 2011, p.174). As with the 1991 film, Scorsese had the screenwriter on set throughout production to revise scenes and develop the lead female character, Vera Farmiga's police psychiatrist (Wilson, 2011, p.272).

Both Max Cady and Jack Nicholson's diabolical mob boss Frank Costello are shown listening to Gaetano Donizetti's tragic opera *Lucia di Lammermoor*. While not possessing Cady's apparent supernatural qualities, Costello is equally Satanic, his Mephisophelean beard and reference to "non serviam" being clues. Nicholson's monster is Satan after the fall, targeting adolescents and corrupting them with a greed only crime can satiate. Costello also has lycanthropic tendencies, gifting a *Wolverine* comic to a young lad who will later become his mole within the Boston Police Department, played by Matt Damon. Both Cady and Leonardo DiCaprio's conflicted undercover cop, Billy Costigan, inherit $30,000 after their mothers die. This enables them to conduct their missions without a regular source of income (Billy attempts to collect his salary after the assignment is complete). As we have seen, the Aramaic word for informer translates as "to eat the flesh of someone else", harkening back to Cady's cannibalistic tendencies.

In title and form, *The Departed* carries overtones of Gothic and horror. Frequently indulged is Scorsese's fondness for incorporating bold splashes of red across his visuals. Costello is part gangster, part Herschell Gordon Lewis throwback, casually producing a dismembered hand at the breakfast table, and emerging from a backroom meeting drenched in gore. Two gangsters are from Providence, birthplace of H.P. Lovecraft, and whose name means, "God's protection". In a subtle display of Frank's dark power, the two mobsters do not last long. There is even reference to Nathaniel Hawthorne's *The House of the Seven Gables* in Billy's paraphrase, "Families are always rising or falling in America."

The meta-commentary deepened in 2019 with Quentin Tarantino's *Once Upon a Time in Hollywood*. Within the layered haze of this cinematic séance is *The Departed*'s Leonardo DiCaprio, playing faded TV star Rick Dalton. Briefly seen is a moment from Dalton's *The Fourteen Fists of McCluskey*, a (fake) World War 2 exploitation movie resembling Enzo G. Castellari's *The Inglorious Bastards* (1978), from which Tarantino had paraphrased the title for his own 2008 film. Accompanying Dalton flambéing Nazi generals is 'The Killing', that cue from Bernard Herrmann's unused *Torn Curtain* score reorchestrated for the climax of *Cape Fear*. From what we see of *The Fourteen Fists of McCluskey*, a hero also torches villains, although the Nazis seem less invulnerable to fire than Max Cady. The fabric of Hollywood's past is once more wrapped around a work that itself reframes and comments upon decades of genre filmmaking.

Almost twenty years would pass before Scorsese tackled horror as directly as in *Cape Fear*. Before then the genre continued to influence his work, sometimes in unlikely places. *Kundun* features a shot lifted from Mario Bava's *Blood and Black Lace*. Describing this moment in a *Sight and Sound* interview, Scorsese's enthusiasm for the aesthetic pleasures of horror shines through: "And of course, the puff of blood coming into the fishpond is this incredible moment in Mario Bava's *Blood and Black Lace* (1964) [*laughs fiendishly*], when the woman is in the bathtub and she's dead and she's got black hair, a white face, and bright red lips, and it's a white bathtub and this blood pumps up" (Taubin, 1998, p.11).

Elaine and Saul Bass' opening credits for 1995's *Casino* recall Satan's expulsion from Heaven, as De Niro's character tumbles through a neon-drenched inferno. The Basses also created the opening credits for 1993's *The Age of Innocence*, Scorsese's next film after *Cape Fear* and more connected than one would expect. As Annette Wernblad notes, the title sequence is set to a piece from Charles Francois Gounod's *Faust*, based on the classic tale of one man's battle with a diabolical tormentor/corruptor. "By implication then, *The Age of Innocence* picks up exactly where *Cape Fear* left off" (2011, p.161). Michelle Pfeiffer plays a figure from lawyer Daniel Day-Lewis' past, returning years later to reveal his weakness and disrupting his comfortable society lifestyle, albeit in less lurid and violent fashion. Infidelity once more hangs heavy in the air, and Day-Lewis' betrothed, played by Winona Ryder, is wholly aware of her husband's wandering eye.

Day-Lewis would join the Scorsese pantheon of Satanic villains with his portrayal of William "Bill the Butcher" Cutting in *Gangs of New York*. Prince of Darkness parallels here are as subtle as one of the headbutts Bill delivers to Leonardo DiCaprio's vengeance-seeking Amsterdam. Before going to war with Bill's gang and being slain at Bill's hand, Amsterdam's father Priest Vallon (Liam Neeson) recounts to his young son the story of St. Michael, the angel who cast Satan from Heaven. Returning to seek revenge as an adult, Amsterdam discovers Bill now has governance over Paradise Square, centre of an area known as the Five Points (i.e. a pentagram). Doubling down on the analogy, Bill's office of business is informally known as 'Satan's Circus'. Cutting shares Cady's fondness for fire, being associated with flame and smoke, annually celebrating his victory over Vallon by imbibing ignited alcohol.

Religion-inflected horrors manifest in the Dantesque tortures inflicted upon Japanese Catholics and Italian priests in *Silence*. *The Irishman*'s Cain and Abel plotting is in keeping with Scorsese's 'too much Good Friday, not enough Easter Sunday' storytelling, although in *The Irishman*, De Niro's Frank Sheeran and Al Pacino's Jimmy Hoffa are both so corrupt it is difficult to tell who is the dark reflection of whom. But within the film's moral framework, Sheeran slaying his union 'brother' is ultimately worse. In *The Wolf of Wall Street*'s orgy scenes we smell a whiff of the sulfur that hung over the religious hysteria in Ken Russell's *The Devils* (1971), and Leonardo DiCaprio's Jordan Belfort is the big bad wolf of post-2008 recession movies.

But Scorsese's two films after *Cape Fear* that most consciously work horror into their aesthetic and plotting are 1999's *Bringing Out the Dead* and 2010's *Shutter Island*.

Reteaming Scorsese with Paul Schrader as screenwriter, *Bringing Out the Dead* reworks *Taxi Driver*'s themes, the difference being that Nicolas Cage's tortured paramedic, Frank Pierce, turns his spiritual anguish inwards rather than outwards. This depiction of early-1990s New York is perhaps even more Dantesque than in the 1976 movie. There are no child prostitutes, but pregnant hookers haunt urban wastelands, limbless homeless crawl the streets, a weeping woman is bathed in red light. An old man who hangs between life and death taunts Frank seemingly from limbo, and the paramedic is similarly haunted by the ghost of a young homeless girl he was unable to save. The Devil has the best tunes, and Scorsese sets this frequently funny Divine Comedy to an eclectic selection of rock n' roll, Motown, classical and punk, along with original cues supplied by *Cape Fear* and *The Age of Innocence* composer Elmer Bernstein.

A nocturnal movie (daylight is first seen 33-minutes into the runtime), *Bringing Out the Dead* is replete with horror tropes and references. A paramedic refers to one particularly hectic shift as "Night of the Living Cheerleaders", while characters are often spattered with blood (other people's and their own), sometimes too resigned to wash it off. A drug hallucination sequence sees Frank pulling the ghosts of those he could not save out of the pavement. Real life, however, keeps pulling the anguished paramedic below ground, and staircases only spiral downwards.

Leonardo DiCaprio's delusional Andrew Laeddis walks *up* a spiral staircase towards the end of *Shutter Island*, but still winds up in a hell of his own making. The film opens with Laeddis regarding his tortured visage in a mirror, while taking a boat journey across choppy waters to an asylum for the criminally insane. We know he does not stand a chance. Laeddis believes he is US Marshall Teddy Daniels, charged with finding a missing patient. In reality he is searching for himself, the investigation a radical roleplay designed to bring the one-time lawman out of his delusion. This being a Scorsese horror movie, realisation leads homewards for a devastating reveal of infanticide and mercy killing.

The ominous atmosphere of Val Lewton films hangs over *Shutter Island*, particularly the storm-swept denouement to *Isle of the Dead*, and the polite malevolence of the urbane cultists in *The 7th Victim* (Robson, 1943). That staircase Laeddis climbs is straight out of Robert Wise's *The Haunting*. Bloody visions of murderous chaos quote *The Shining*, and Scorsese employs pieces by Polish composer Krzysztof Penderecki, whose music Kubrick used extensively in his horror film. The split-personality reveal, present in Lehane's novel, has become such a cliché it is frustrating how long *Shutter Island* takes to confirm what everyone knows is going on. Subsequent viewings, when the audience can enjoy the Gothic atmosphere and ripe performances without distraction, improve the film. One such performance is delivered by Elias Koteas, cameoing as a frightening figment of Laeddis' imagination, and bearing a remarkable resemblance to De Niro's creature in *Frankenstein*.

Like *Bringing Out the Dead*, *Shutter Island*'s world is a hellscape, where violence is an innate part of the human condition. Set in the early 1950s, Laeddis is plagued by memories of liberating Dachau, and atomic paranoia looms like an invisible mushroom cloud. As warden Ted Levine, *The Silence of the Lambs*' Buffalo Bill, tells Laeddis, "God loves violence… God gave us violence to wage in his honour." These are sentiments of which Max Cady would approve. As with Travis Bickle and Jake La Motta, Laeddis is his own dark shadow, and his horror at discovering a propensity for the Lord's gift makes him "God's lonely man".

As with *Cape Fear*, controversy would surround the releases of *The Wolf of Wall Street* and *The Irishman*. At an AMPAS screening of *The Wolf of Wall Street*, Scorsese was berated by an unnamed screenwriter who reportedly yelled, "Shame on you" (Child, 2013). As with *Goodfellas*, the film drew ire for supposedly glamourising the lead character's amoral lifestyle, and was criticised for depicting a commodification of women by its male characters. As previously mentioned, Anna Paquin's near wordless performance in *The Irishman* was declared further proof that Scorsese was uninterested in engaging female roles. That film's producer, Emma Tillinger Koskoff, argued against this and cited female characters in numerous Scorsese films, including *Cape Fear*'s Leigh and Danielle, as proof the director is "…responsible for some of the greatest female characters in cinema history" (Itzkoff, 2020).

THE END…

Three decades after its release, *Cape Fear* seems less commercial and more Scorsese than it did in 1991. A dearth of sympathetic characters was recognisably part of the filmmaker's M.O., as was the film's lack of interest in being likeable popcorn fare. But, there is a relentlessness to its dread unbalanced by the absence of an audience anchor akin to, for example, Clarice Starling. We have reviewed how Scorsese adapted the remake to fit his themes, and for fans of the director there is pleasure in seeing him transform a solid thriller into a tragedy of spiritual anguish and terror. Scorsese's feature films during the noughties – *Gangs of New York*, *The Aviator*, *The Departed* – had an anonymity to them that made the bravura filmmaking here a reminder of his masterly use of form. *Shutter Island* began a return to more visually interesting work, while *Hugo* (2011) and *The Wolf of Wall Street* are vintage Scorsese in their directorial dynamism. With *Silence* and *The Irishman*, he has developed a more contemplative camera that nonetheless remains diverting.

Despite the criticism of *Cape Fear*'s sexual politics, Emma Tillinger Koskoff is correct in saying Leigh and Danielle are amongst the most interesting female characters in Scorsese's filmography. As noted, this has as much to do with what the actors brought to the picture as what he was interested in exploring. Lange and Lewis' performances demonstrate that a film is more than the input of just the director, no matter how personal a stamp said director puts on their work.

Scorsese has continued his appreciation of horror into the twenty-first century, championing a movie that uses the genre to dramatise familial trauma in ways that crossover with *Cape Fear*. Ari Aster's *Hereditary* (2018) is an unequivocally supernatural tale, but the trauma emerges from a painful family dynamic. In a discussion during 2019's 57th New York Film Festival, Scorsese commented, "The actual supernatural plot to it I remember of course… but, what I really think is powerful in the film is really the family dynamic" (video quote in Raup, 2020). Through Aster's approach on *Hereditary*, Scorsese sees a continuation of horror from the classical period into modern cinema, comparing the picture to films on his list of eleven: "It reminds me of the best of the horror of the Val Lewton films… I don't say it's made the same way, but it's elevated up to like *The Changeling*, *The Haunting*, *The Innocents*" (video quote in Raup, 2020). Scorsese's description of how horror is deployed in Aster's debut feature echoes his use of the genre on *Cape Fear*. "The horror aspects of it, they shock you in a good way, I think. They shock you into a kind of awakening, in a way, of the real pain of these people" (video quote in Raup, 2020).

In 2019, the director courted controversy with a whole new generation of cinemagoers when he told *Empire* magazine that Marvel films were not cinema. In *The New York Times*, he wrote, "They are sequels in name but they are remakes in spirit…" (Scorsese,

2019). A warmer re-evaluation of *Cape Fear* on his part thus seems unlikely. Scorsese's chief contention was that the homogenising effect of franchise filmmaking narrowed cinema's potential. "What's not there is revelation, mystery or genuine emotional risk" (Scorsese, 2019). These, I would argue, are all present in his remake of *Cape Fear*, and his articulation of them is what makes it one of his most successful pictures – that, and a delirium not often found outside the cinema of Dario Argento or Ken Russell.

After all, how many films could get away with a Götterdämmerung action climax in which a Satanic villain asks the nominal hero, "Can you please quote for me the American Bar Association's Rules of Professional Conduct, canon 7?"

Fig. 20

Bibliography

Anderson, Ariston, (2019) 'Martin Scorsese Laments "Young People's" Understanding of Cinema, Shoots Down Question on Lack of Female Characters' *The Hollywood Reporter*, 21st October 2019. Online. Available at https://www.hollywoodreporter.com/news/rome-martin-scorsese-laments-young-peoples-understanding-cinema-1248997 [Accessed 29 April 2021]

Atkinson, Michael (2013) 'Southern Gothic' *Gothic – The Dark Heart of Film*. James Bell (ed) London, BFI

Bettelheim, Bruno (1975) *The Uses of Enchantment*. London; Penguin

Bouzereau, Laurent (1995) *The Making of Jaws*. Universal Home Video

Bouzereau, Laurent (2001) *The Making of Cape Fear*. Universal Home Video

Bouzereau, Laurent (2001) *The Making of Cape Fear* [1962]. Universal Home Video

Bordwell, David (2006) 'The Departed: No departure' *David Bordwell's Website on Cinema*. Online. Available at http://www.davidbordwell.net/blog/2006/10/10/the-departed-no-departure/ [Accessed 29 April 2021]

Cherry, Brigid (2009) *Horror*. Abingdon, Routledge

Child, Ben (2013) 'Martin Scorsese heckled at Academy screening of The Wolf of Wall Street' *The Guardian* - 23 Dec 2013. Online. Available at https://www.theguardian.com/film/2013/dec/23/martin-scorsese-heckled-wolf-of-wall-street-screening-sex-drugs [Accessed 29 April 2021]

Chisholm, Hugh, ed. (1911), 'Angelus Silesius' *Encyclopedia Britannica*, 2 (11th ed.), Cambridge University Press

Clover, Carol J. (1992) *Men, Women, and Chain Saws*. London, BFI

Douglas, Illeana (2017) 'Illeana Douglas on Cape Fear' *Trailers From Hell*. Online Available at https://www.youtube.com/watch?v=XP9HKM7rVNE [Accessed 29 April 2021]

Ebert, Roger (1991) Cape Fear review *Siskel & Ebert*. Online. Available at https://www.youtube.com/watch?v=t6eBK4fchnU [Accessed 29 April 2021]

Ebert, Roger (2008) *Scorsese by Ebert*. Chicago; The University of Chicago Press

'Who's Afraid of Cape Fear' *Empire* 32 (February 1992) (author uncredited)

Gleiberman, Owen (1992) 'Happy Families?...' *Empire* 33 (March 1992)

Grant, Barry Keith (1998) 'Rich and strange: the yuppie horror film' *Contemporary Hollywood Cinema*. Neale, Steve & Smith, Murray (eds) London, Routledge

Greven David (2013) *Psycho-Sexual: Male Desire in Hitchcock, de Palma, Scorsese and Friedkin*. Texas, University of Texas Press

Grubb, Davis (1953) *The Night of the Hunter*. Vintage Books, New York (2015 edition)

The Holy Bible. London, Trinitarian Bible Society

Itzkoff, Dave (2020) 'Martin Scorsese is Letting Go' *The New York Times*, 2 Jan 2020 (updated 31 Jan 2020). Online. Available at https://www.nytimes.com/2020/01/02/movies/martin-scorsese-irishman.html [Accessed 29 April 2021]

Hawthorne, Nathaniel (1851) *The House of the Seven Gables*. Aerie Books Ltd. NYC (1988 edition)

Hoberman, J. (1992) 'Sacred and Profane' *Sight and Sound* Vol.1 Issue 10

Kernes, Mark (July 2014). "Fear' Factor, Bonnie gets her DeNiro on for Dreamzone' *Adult Video News*. Vol. 31 no. 7. p. 42

Klawans, Stuart (1991) 'Cape Fear' review *The Free Library*. Online. Available at https://www.thefreelibrary.com/Cape+Fear-a011693083 [Accessed 29 April 2021]

Levy, Shawn (2014) *De Niro: A Life*. New York; Three Rivers Press

Lovecraft, H.P. (1927) *Supernatural Horror in Literature*. Online. Available at https://www.hplovecraft.com/writings/texts/essays/shil.aspx [Accessed 29 April 2021]

MacDonald, John (1957) *Cape Fear*. London; Penguin

Janet Maslin (1991) 'Martin Scorsese Ventures Back to Cape Fear' *The New York Times*, Nov 10, 1991

Mueller, Matt (1992) 'Cape Fear' review *Empire* 33 (March 1992)

Monléon, Jose (1990) *A Specter is Haunting Europe*. New Jersey, Princeton University Press

Morgan, David (1991a) 'On Location: Back to Cape Fear" *Los Angeles Times*, 17 Feb 1991. Online. Available at https://www.latimes.com/archives/la-xpm-1991-02-17-ca-1842-story.html [Accessed 29 April 2021]

David Morgan (1991b) 'Cinematographer Freddie Francis on Shooting Cape Fear' *Wide Angle/CloseUp*. Online. Available at http://www.wideanglecloseup.com/francis.html [Accessed 29 April 2021]

Morgan, David (1991c) 'Interview with Wesley Strick' *Wide Angle/CloseUp*. Online. Available at http://www.wideanglecloseup.com/strick.html [Accessed 29 April 2021]

Morgan, David (1991d) 'Interview with Editor Thelma Schoonmaker' *Wide Angle/CloseUp*. Online. Available at http://www.wideanglecloseup.com/schoonmaker.html [Accessed 29 April 2021]

Morgan, David (1992) 'F-C-B-F Spells Fear' *Empire* 33 (March 1992)

Neale, Steve (2000) *Genre and Hollywood*. London, Routledge

Newman, Kim (2011) *Nightmare Movies: Horror On Screen Since the 1960s*. London, Bloomsbury

Norman, Barry (1962), 'Film chief censors Our 'Erb' *Daily Mail*, 13 June 1962

Norman, Barry (1992) *Film '92 Films of the Year* Online. Available at https://www.youtube.com/watch?v=AnhBzN3q_2M [Accessed 29 April 2021]

O'Brien, Catherine (2018) *Martin Scorsese's Divine Comedy*. London, Bloomsbury

O'Neal, Sean (2009) 'Illeana Douglas' *AV Club*. Available at https://film.avclub.com/illeana-douglas-1798215702 [Accessed 29 April 2021]

Power, Ed (2018) 'Steven Spielberg's year of living dangerously: How he reinvented cinema with Jurassic Park and Schindler's List' *The Independent*, 28 November 2018. Online. Available at https://www.independent.co.uk/arts-entertainment/films/news/steven-spielberg-schindlers-list-25th-anniversary-jurassic-park-martin-scorsese-a8655561.html [Accessed 29 April 2021]

Rafferty, Terrence (1991) 'Cape Fear' *The New Yorker*. Online. Available at https://scrapsfromtheloft.com/2017/10/25/cape-fear-1991-review-by-terrence-rafferty-the-new-yorker/ [Accessed 29 April 2021]

Raup, Jordan (2020) 'Cinema Stories: Martin Scorsese on the Unforgettable Horror of *Hereditary*' Film at Lincoln Center. Available at https://www.filmlinc.org/daily/cinema-stories-martin-scorsese-on-the-unforgettable-horror-of-hereditary/ [Accessed 29th April 2021]

Read, Jacinda (2000) *The New Avengers: Feminism, femininity and the rape-revenge cycle.* Manchester, Manchester University Press

Reidy, Tim (2012) 'Martin Scorsese Responds to "America" Essay *America – The Jesuit Review*. Available at https://www.americamagazine.org/content/all-things/martin-scorsese-responds-america-essay [Accessed 29 April 2021]

Rosenbaum, Jonathan (1991) 'Cape Fear' review *Chicago Reader*. Online. Available at https://www.jonathanrosenbaum.net/2020/12/bag-of-tics-the-1991-cape-fear/ [Accessed 29 April 2021]

Schickel, Richard (2011) *Conversations with Scorsese*. New York, Alfred A. Knopf

Scorsese, Martin (1976) *Taxi Driver* (audio commentary). Sony Pictures Home Entertainment UK (2011)

'Martin Scorsese on Letterman, February 18, 1982' *Late Night with David Letterman*. Online. Available at https://www.youtube.com/watch?v=qmLlqWCVGJ8 [Accessed 29 April 2021]

Scorsese, Martin (1985) *After Hours* (audio commentary). Warner Bros. Entertainment Inc. (2004)

Scorsese, Martin (2019) 'Martin Scorsese: I Said Marvel Movies Aren't Cinema. Let Me Explain.' *The New York Times*, 4 Nov 2019. Online. Available at https://www.nytimes.com/2019/11/04/opinion/martin-scorsese-marvel.html [Accessed 29 April 2021]

Shelley, Mary (1818) *Frankenstein, or The Modern Prometheus*. London, Penguin (2003 edition of revised 1831 text)

Shone, Tom (2014) *Scorsese: A Retrospective*. London, Thames & Hudson

Stevenson, Robert Louis (1886), *The Strange Case of Dr Jekyll and Mr Hyde*. Online. Public domain version available through Apple's 'Books' app, p.24 in iPad portrait mode

Stern, Lesley (1995) *The Scorsese Connection*. London, BFI

Strick, Wesley (1990) *Cape Fear – August 31, 1990*. Online. Available at https://scripts-onscreen.com/movie/cape-fear-script-links/ [Accessed 29 April 2021]

Taubin, Amy (1991) 'Killing Men' *Sight and Sound* Vol.1, Issue 1

Taubin, Amy (1998) 'Everything is Form' *Sight and Sound* Vol.8, Issue 2

Taubin, Amy (2000) *Taxi Driver*. London, BFI

Thompson, David/Christie, Ian (1989) *Scorsese on Scorsese*. London, Faber and Faber

Thompson, David/Christie, Ian (1996) *Scorsese on Scorsese* (revised edition). London, Faber and Faber

Tudor, Andrew (1989) *Monsters and Mad Scientists: A Cultural History of the Horror Movie*. Oxford, Basil Blackwell

Wernblad, Annette (2011) *The Passion of Martin Scorsese*. North Carolina, McFarland

Wilson, Lena (2021) 'Rape-Revenge Tales: Cathartic? Maybe. Incomplete? Definitely.' *The New York Times*, 14 Jan 2021. Online. Available at https://www.nytimes.com/2021/01/14/movies/rape-revenge-films-flaws.html [Accessed 29 April 2021]

Wilson, Michael Henry (2011) *Scorsese on Scorsese*. Paris; Cahiers du Cinema

Wood, Robin (1986) *Hollywood from Vietnam to Reagan*. New York, Columbia University Press

Wood, Robin (2003) *Hollywood from Vietnam to Reagan… and Beyond*. New York, Columbia University Press

DEVIL'S ADVOCATES

"Auteur Publishing's new Devil's Advocates critiques on individual titles offer bracingly fresh perspectives from passionate writers. The series will perfectly complement the BFI archive volumes." Christopher Fowler, Independent on Sunday

BLOOD AND BLACK LACE – ROBERTO CURTI

"From rare production details to forensic analysis of Bava's masterful camerawork and colour, you couldn't ask for a more authoritative study of this seminal giallo." – Leon Hunt, Brunel University

FRENZY – IAN COOPER

"With excellent diversions and delvings, this is a smart, thoroughly entertaining reassessment of Hitchcock's most divisive film. Repellent and misogynistic or a black comic masterpiece? Like all good film books, it makes you want to watch it again. And again." – Stephen Volk, screenwriter (Ghostwatch, Gothic, The Awakening)

PEEPING TOM – KIRI BLOOM WALDEN

"...a thorough and incredibly well researched book... Informative, concise and passionately and intelligently argued, it will make you appreciate Peeping Tom in a whole new light." – Frightfest.co.uk

www.ingramcontent.com/pod-product-compliance
Lightning Source LLC
Chambersburg PA
CBHW071413300426
44114CB00016B/2285